Dear Betty:-
Love,
Edith

Dear Betty:-
Love,
Edith

*Letters and secret thoughts
from a Minneapolis ingénue
while a Wellesley student in 1916,
a nurse's aide in Paris during World War I,
a newlywed in Prohibition Chicago,
and a Pasadena divorcée*

Compiled by
Mary Ames Mitchell

Peach Plum Press
San Rafael, California

Compiled and edited by
Mary Ames Mitchell – Edith's granddaughter
Partially transcribed by
Elizabeth Winter Ames   Edith's granddaughter
Edited by
Leila Dean Jackson Poullada – Betty's daughter
Additional comments by
Catharine Ames Jackson Wise – Betty's daughter
Mary Ames Wolff – Betty's niece

•

The letters from Edith Ames Winter Ames McGinnis
to her first cousin Elizabeth Ames Jackson
were copied and printed with permission from
the Ames Family Historical Collection in Boulder, Colorado,
where they were archived.
Executive Director, Linda Ames Cowan
Board President, Mary Ames Wolff

•

The collection has since moved to the Schlesinger Library
at Radcliffe College in Cambridge, Massachusetts.
www.radcliffe.harvard.edu/news/schlesinger-newsletter/
many-families-one-collection.

•

Peach Plum Press
Published in San Rafael, California, 94901
www.MaryAmesMitchell.com

•

ISBN Print Hardback: 978-0-9850530-6-2
ISBN Print Paperback: 978-0-9850530-7-9
ISBN eBook: 978-0-9850530-5-5
Library of Congress Control Number: 2017932308

Hats off to Mary Ames Wolff for rescuing these documents from the attic of 501 Grand.

•

*To the Schlesinger Library
for taking care of them now.*

•

*To Mary's daughter, Linda Cowan,
for arranging for me to see and copy the letters
for this publication.*

•

*To Betty's daughters, Leila and Kitty, and to
my cousin Liz, for your assistance and support.*

Contents

Minneapolis and St. Paul

※

On March 5, 1990, in St. Paul, Minnesota, ninety-six-year-old Elizabeth Ames Jackson – known by her close family as 'Betty' – passed away and left her home at 501 Grand Avenue to the next generation. The third floor was so large that in earlier times, it served as an entertainment center for Betty and her five siblings when they produced family plays. Betty was the last one of those siblings to "pass on to the next stage." Her husband, Norris Dean Jackson, followed six months later.

Betty's niece, Mary Ames Wolff, rescued box-loads of letters that were taking space in the attics and innumerable closets. Some of the papers in those boxes had been in the attic for decades; some for over a century. Mary transported them to her home in Colorado and paid a professional librarian to sort, organize and archive them properly. The project took nearly twenty years. Meanwhile, word got out that the documents contained important, historical and fascinating information.

In San Francisco, I, Edith Mary Ames Mitchell, was searching for records about my paternal grandmother, Edith Ames Winter, who had been Betty's first cousin. My grandmother died when I was fourteen. I did not know that anything personally written by her still existed. I remembered my mother receiving letters that she had written on blue Crane stationery. But my mother did not keep those letters, and other memories of my grandmother were vague and few.

Edith was one year younger than Betty. Betty was the closest thing Edith had to a best friend. When I learned from my Uncle Bob Ames (Edith's youngest son), who had learned from his second-cousin Kitty Ames Wise (Betty's youngest daughter) that among the documents Betty had stored in her attic were the letters Edith had written to her during their lifetimes, I flew to Colorado to read them.

I took the opportunity to snap photos of the letters with my digital camera. When I returned to California, I transcribed them with the help of my first cousin Elizabeth Winter Ames. Edith had nine grandchildren: six girls and three boys. We all loved her very much.

The abbreviated family tree below describes Edith and Betty's relationship to each other. Betty was the only one who did not have a middle name.

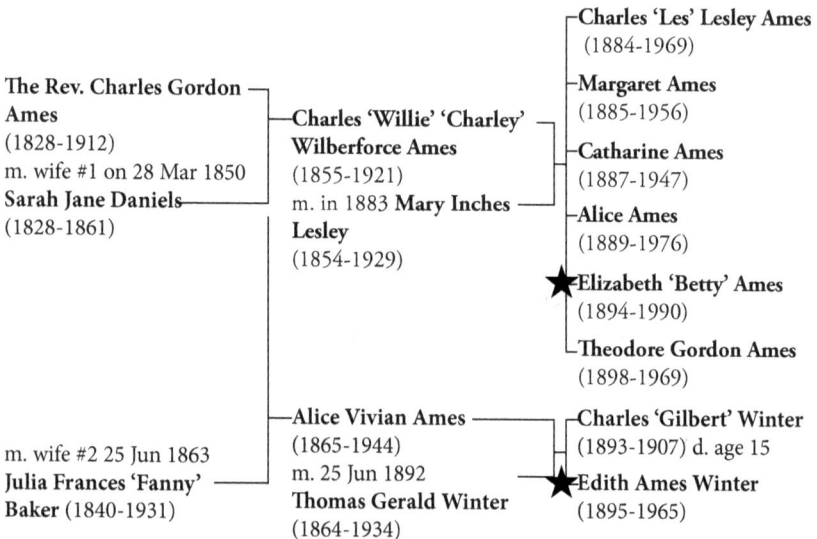

The Rev. Charles Gordon Ames (1828-1912)
m. wife #1 on 28 Mar 1850 Sarah Jane Daniels (1828-1861)

— Charles 'Willie' 'Charley' Wilberforce Ames (1855-1921)
m. in 1883 Mary Inches Lesley (1854-1929)

- Charles 'Les' Lesley Ames (1884-1969)
- Margaret Ames (1885-1956)
- Catharine Ames (1887-1947)
- Alice Ames (1889-1976)
- ★Elizabeth 'Betty' Ames (1894-1990)
- Theodore Gordon Ames (1898-1969)

m. wife #2 25 Jun 1863 Julia Frances 'Fanny' Baker (1840-1931)

— Alice Vivian Ames (1865-1944)
m. 25 Jun 1892 Thomas Gerald Winter (1864-1934)

- Charles 'Gilbert' Winter (1893-1907) d. age 15
- ★Edith Ames Winter (1895-1965)

Edith's mother, Alice Vivian Ames, was the half sister of Betty's father, Charles Wilberforce Ames. Edith and Betty had different grandmothers. Their mutual grandfather, Charles Gordon Ames, married Edith's grandmother, Fanny Baker, two years after Betty's grandmother, Sarah Daniels, died. Fanny became the mother of the house when Charles Wilberforce was eight. She served as paternal grandmother for Charles' six children, including Betty.

I want Edith to tell her own story. However, I have filled in factual information and my own memories to help that story make sense. Betty's daughters, Leila Poullada and Kitty Wise – both in their nineties – have added their memories. Kitty lives in Rochester, New York. Leila lives in St. Paul not far from 501 Grand where this story began.

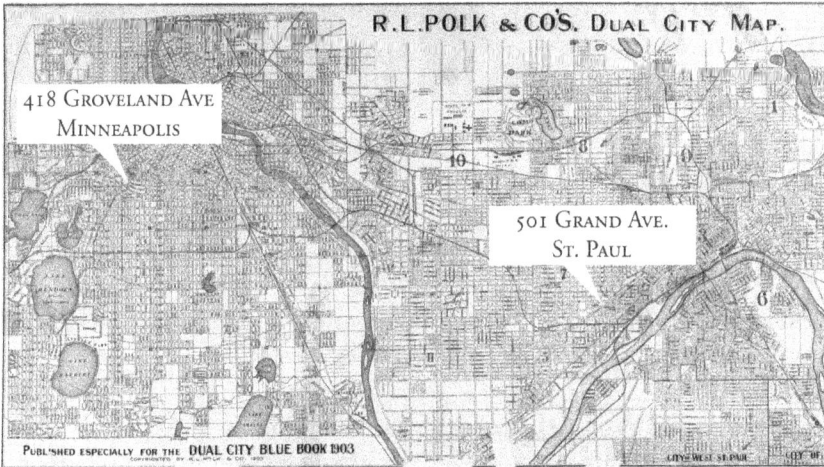

R.L.POLK & CO'S. DUAL CITY MAP.

418 GROVELAND AVE
MINNEAPOLIS

501 GRAND AVE.
ST. PAUL

PUBLISHED ESPECIALLY FOR THE DUAL CITY BLUE BOOK 1903

Edith was born on December 7, 1895, in Minneapolis, Minnesota, across the Mississippi River from St. Paul, where her one-year-old cousin Betty lived. The map above was drafted in 1903 when Edith was eight and Betty was nine. Later, as teenagers, they traveled to each other's houses on horse-drawn street cars.

Alice, Edith and Tom Winter, 1896.

Edith had one sibling, a brother three years older named Gilbert.

On June 4, 1907, when Edith was twelve, fifteen-year-old Gilbert and his closest friend, Eric Passmore, were home alone at the Winter's residence in Minneapolis. Edith and Gilbert's mother, Alice, was away on a business trip. Their father, Tom, was at their summer home on Lake Minnetonka. While rummaging around Gilbert's father's desk, the boys came upon a .38 caliber Smith & Weston revolver. They decided to examine it.

Gilbert had been well versed by his father on how to use a gun. They often hunted together. According to the newspaper clipping, "Gilbert left the room for a moment while Eric was in the act of trying the revolver. It is said that Eric did not know the weapon was loaded and accidentally allowed the hammer to fall just as his friend came back into the room. The weapon was discharged, raising it slightly, which sent the bullet to Gilbert's breast. Gilbert fell to the floor with a wound to the right side of his breast [through his lung] and died instantly." Gilbert's cousin Betty saved the following news articles.

BOY KILLS PLAYMATE

FATAL ACCIDENT IN MILL CITY.

Lads Find Revolver and Weapon Is Discharged During Play—Gilbert Winter Killed.

Gilbert Winter, the thirteen-year-old son of Mr. and Mrs. T. G. Winter, 418 Groveland avenue, Minneapolis, was shot and killed last evening by his playmate, Eric Passmore, the thirteen-year-old son of Mr. and Mrs. William Passmore, 233 Oak Grove street.

The boys were at the Winter residence. Mrs. Winter is in the East and Mr. Winter was at Lake Minnetonka.

ACCIDENTAL SHOT ENDS BOY'S LIFE

TWO HOMES SADDENED BY A HEARTRENDING TRAGEDY.

Gilbert Winter, While Entertaining His Friend Eric Passmore, Killed by Discharge of Revolver in Playmate's Hands—Surviving Lad Crushed by Grief.

Gilbert Winter, 15 years old, was accidentally shot and instantly killed last night in his father's home, 418 Groveland avenue, by Eric Passmore,

TWO HOMES SADDENED BY A HEARTRENDING TRAGEDY.

Gilbert Winter, While Entertaining His Friend Eric Passmore, Killed by Discharge of Revolver in Playmate's Hands—Surviving Lad Crushed by Grief.

Gilbert Winter, 15 years old, was accidentally shot and instantly killed last night in his father's home, 418 Groveland avenue, by Eric Passmore, his closest friend, who accidentally pulled the trigger of a revolver while examining the firearm.

Grief-stricken over the accident, Eric Passmore today is a nervous wreck and requires almost constant

By all accounts, Gilbert and his sister were extremely close. Gilbert's death left Edith an only child. She turned to Betty as a pseudo sister.

Both Edith's parents and Betty's parents were prominent citizens in their communities. Edith's mother, Alice, had been born in Albany, New York. She obtained her undergraduate and graduate degrees from Wellesley College. "She was the first one to achieve a perfect score on the final classics exam," said her youngest grandson, my Uncle Bob (Robert Dawes Ames). Alice was well known for her charity work. My father, Thomas Winter Ames, who was Edith's middle son, called his Grandmother Alice "a professional do-gooder."

Edith's father, Thomas Gerald Winter (after whom my father was named), was British. The eighteenth child of the former mayor of Grantham, England, who was also named Thomas Winter, Thomas had migrated to America through Canada, where he served for a short period as a mounted Canadian policeman. He settled in America's wheat capital, Minneapolis, established a business owning grain elevators and helped found Minneapolis' park system.

Betty is the petite blonde sitting on her mother's left knee. The baby is Teddy.

Betty grew up in the 501 Grand Avenue residence in St. Paul. Her daughter Kitty wrote, "Mummy was one of six children. In order, they were: Charles ('Lesley'), Margaret, Catharine, Alice, Mummy and Theodore." Four girls were bracketed by two boys. Edith will mention Betty's siblings frequently.

According to Betty's daughter Kitty, her mother and her youngest brother, Teddy, were particularly close. "Ted was born exactly four years after Mummy's birth. The story goes that my four-year-old mother sat at breakfast on the morning of her birthday wondering why her mother had not arrived yet. Her father, my grandfather Charles Wilberforce, told her that her mother was preparing a big present for her birthday. When, several hours later my grandmother arrived from upstairs holding tiny Theodore, Betty thought her new brother was 'hers.' The bond created at that moment lasted the rest of their lives."

Betty and Edith's grandfather, Charles Gordon Ames, named his first child, Charles Wilberforce Ames, after himself and after the famous abolitionist. 'CGA,' as my father (his great-grandson) referred to him, was very involved with the abolition movement as well as women's rights and the prohibition of alcohol. His wife, Fanny, Edith's grandmother, is listed in the *Book of Women's Firsts* by Reed and Witlleb* as a "co-founder with her husband, Charles, of the first visiting social worker service in the United States. ... the Relief Society of Germantown, Pennsylvania, where Charles headed a Unitarian congregation. The society afforded the first opportunity for social workers – actually volunteer women – to visit the urban poor and report on needy cases." Fanny was also the first female factory inspector in Massachusetts. She was trying to help enforce child labor laws.

During his early childhood, Charles Wilberforce was referred to as 'Willie.' At age ten, he insisted that he be called 'Charles' like his father. He graduated from Cornell University with a bachelors in literature. He worked first as a secretary, then general manager and finally as president of West Publishing Company in St. Paul. The company thrived under his guidance and for many years was the largest publishing house for law books in the world. Like Edith's father, Betty's father was involved with public affairs. He was particularly interested in the library, schools, and in 1908 helped found the St. Paul Institute and the St. Paul Academy (SPA)

Betty's mother, Mary Lesley, was from Milton (thirty-nine miles south of Boston) and also Philadelphia. Mary's father, Professor J. Peter Lesley, was a geologist, a well respected one. The Lesleys were Presbyterians and then became Unitarians. Like Charles Gordon Ames, Peter Lesley supported the abolition movement. Before the Civil War, he and his wife, Susan Inches Lyman Lesley, with the help of others, relocated and housed a fugitive slave.**

Peter and Susan Lesley and Charles G. and Fanny Ames were good friends in Philadelphia. They worked toward mutual causes before their children, Mary and Charles, met and married.

Betty's daughter Leila told me, "Boston and Philadelphia were the cultural centers of America at the time. New England's transcendentalist movement nested there. Ralph Waldo Emerson, Henry David Thoreau and the philosopher Chauncey Wright [1830-1875] were a tight gang. My grandparents were an integral part of that.

---

*Read, Phyllis J. Witlieb, Bernard L. *The Book of Women's Firsts*, Random House, New York, 1992.

**Professor Sydney Nathans of Duke University referenced the Ames Family Collection to publish the story of how Peter and Susan Lesley harbored an escaped slave woman before the Civil War. *To Free a Family: The Journey of Mary Walker*. Harvard University Press, 2012.

By the time Edith began writing these letters to Betty, the Lesleys had
died – Peter Lesley in 1903 and Susan Lesley in 1904. Charles G. and
Fanny Ames still lived in Boston. Charles served as the minister of the
Unitarian Church of the Disciples there.

Edith wrote the first letter two years after her brother Gilbert's
death. She was fourteen years old and Betty was fifteen. Betty had just
had a birthday. Edith used a letterhead from Betty's family home at 501
Grand, where she spent a good deal of time because her mother often
traveled. Her own address was 418 Groveland Avenue in Minneapolis.
Betty was in Boston following in the footsteps of her three older sisters
Margaret, Catharine and Alice by attending Miss Winsor's School.

Mary Pickard Winsor (1860-1950) was a close family friend of the
Ames family in Boston. She founded Miss Winsor's School in 1886 at
her private home on Beacon Hill with eight girls. In 1910, the year after
this letter was written, the school moved to Boston's Fenway with 225
students. Its motto, suggested by President Elliot of Harvard, became "A
sound mind in a sound body." Today, the school is located at 103 Pilgrim
Road and has approximately 432 students. The *Wall Street Journal*
identified it as one of the top fifty schools for preparing students for
American universities.*

Our cover image of Edith and the image below of Betty were taken
about the time Edith's letters commence.

---

*From Wikipedia on the Winsor School: http://en.wikipedia.org/
wiki/Winsor_School

September 17, 1909
Minnesota

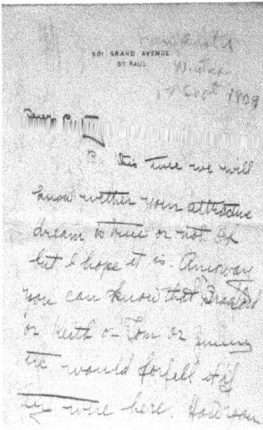

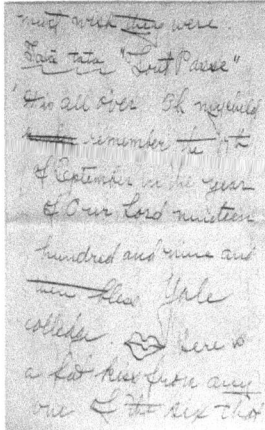

501 GRAND AVENUE, ST. PAUL

Dear Cutey,

By this time we will know wether[sic] your attractive dream is true or not. Oh but I hope it is. Anyway you can know that Bradford or Keith [Merrill*] or Tom or Jimmy etc would forfill[sic] it if they were here. How you must wish they were. Tata Tata "Tout Passa" "It is all over" Oh my child, remember the 17th of September in the year of Our Lord nineteen hundred and nine and then bless Yale college.

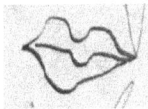

Here is a fat kiss from any one of the six that you choose it to be from. There you stand and talk to Josshapine[sic] about silk dresses and you don't know how I love you. Now you are going to play that for me and I must go and hold your hand.

If you like Janet Lowll[sic] I shall go east and murder her so please don't tell me about her.

Ta ta love
From Edith

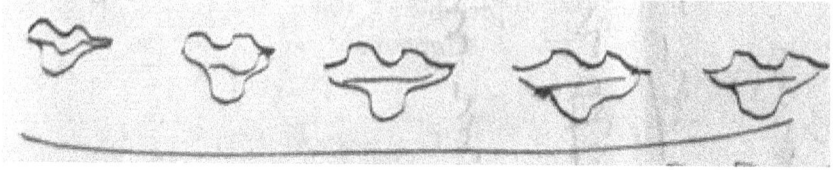

Do you know what these are?

_____

*According to Betty's daughter Leila, Keith Merrill's family were good friends of Betty's family in St. Paul.

Probably **September 1910**
Wintermere, Long Lake, Minnesota

This letter is not dated, however the text helps us identify the time period. Mary Wolff [the daughter of Betty's brother Lesley, known as 'Les'] explained that Edith and Betty were being fitted for Les and Betty's sister Catharine's wedding to Samuel Epes Turner on September 24, 1910. Catharine was six years older than Betty and the first of the six siblings to get married.

The letter is written from Wintermere on Long Lake. My father told me his grandparents, the Winters, owned a house by a lake in Minnesota. However, Edith refers to many lake houses in her letters. Long Lake is nine miles west of the Winter's principal residence at 418 Groveland Avenue and just north of Lake Minnetonka. Wintermere is probably the place where Thomas Winter was when his son Gilbert was shot.

WINTERMERE

P O LONG LAKE, MINN.

RFD No.1

Dear Betty

Please do write my love. I have decided to try Central [High School] and if I do not like it I am to tutor. School begins tomorrow and I am going to stay with Janet Frey till Friday. Next week I am going to spend Tuesday and Wednesday nights at the Trendalls. So if Catharine wants me to be fitted I will have to come in the afternoon and she had better call up father a day or two ahead.

Janet is out here just now but we haven't done anything especial. When I come down to St. Paul I will bring your waist and the underclothes Margaret [Betty's sister] left out here. They are all clean but if they stay much longer I shall wear them. I have a new waist, a copy of yours, but it has a frill down the front like the drawing

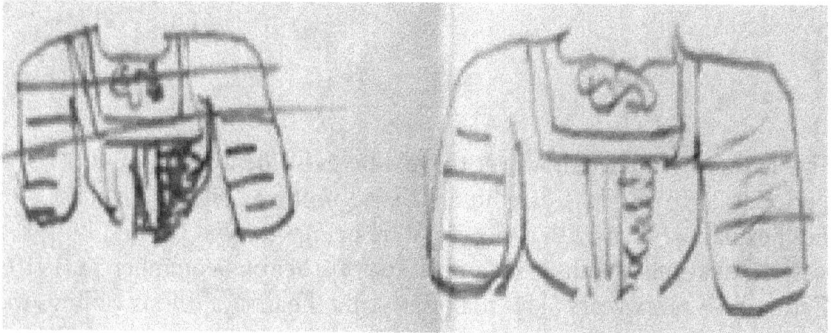

Well ta-ta
Ruby my love to you from your only
Pearl
(Svenson).
P.S. How is Tom Daniels?
P.P.S. How is Keith Merril?
and P.P.P.S. How is Herbert Kennedy?
Is Bud at home yet? Please send me Anne Foley's address if you think she would like to have me write to her.

Today there are two 'Central High' schools in the Twin Cities area: St. Paul Central High School (the oldest high school in Minnesota) and Minneapolis Central High School, which did not open until 1913. Edith, obviously, attended the former.

The 'boys' Edith mentions are friends from the Twin Cities who have 'gone East' for college or college preparatory school. Leila noted that Tom Daniels was a St. Paul friend who, she thinks, went to Yale. Herbert Kennedy was a brother of Walter who later married 'Lib' Dean, a first cousin of Betty's husband Norris Dean Jackson who lived in the Grand Hill neighborhood. "The community was very tightly knit," Leila noted.

January 9, 1910
Central High, Minneapolis, Minnesota

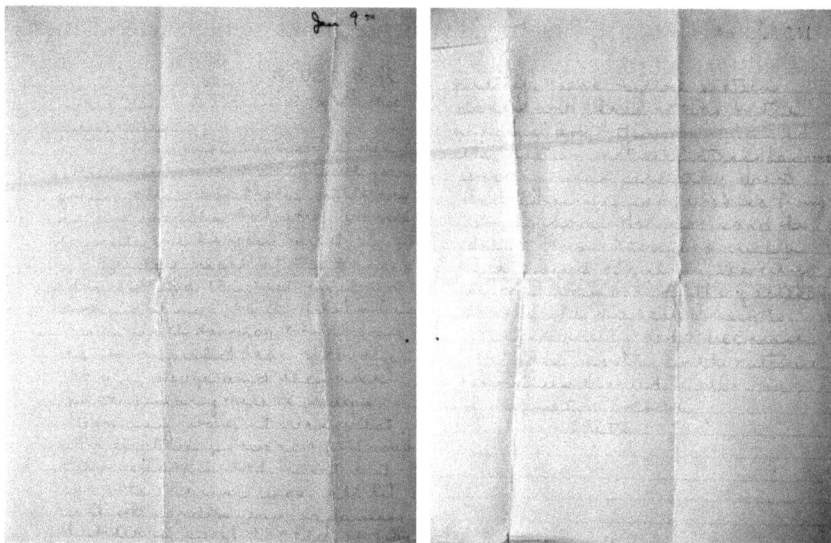

Dearest Betty.

I suppose you are all settled down now and have forgotten all about your little cous in Minneapolis but you promised to write me so you must.

Friday night at the ΠΚΧ dance I had the best time you can imagine. In the first place I went with Harmon Edsall and he is a perfect dear. Secondly I am a pledge and they are particularly nice to pledges. Then anyway it was great. The electric power all through Minneapolis had burnt out so the house was all lit with candles and Japanese lanterns so it looked awfully pretty. There were sixteen dances and three extras on the program but we only danced the sixteen not the extras. Laurence Gregory was perfectly great and Robern Gipson was so funny. Going home Harmon said he didn't know there was such a nice crowd of girls in the city and it was one of the greatest dances he had ever been to. That is pretty good because he goes mostly with Katherine Durnnell's crowd. Well — me for Latin have.* Edith

---

*Edith is mimicking the Latin sentence structure.

Fall, 1910
Minneapolis

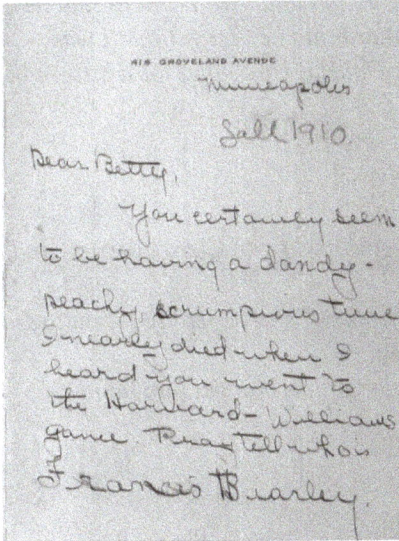

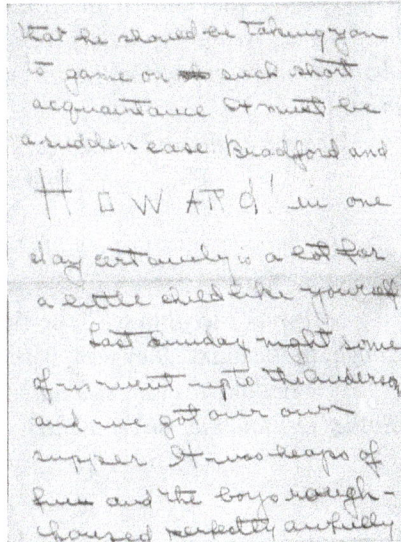

418 GROVELAND AVENUE

Dear Betty,

You certainly seem to be having a dandy-peachy, scrumptious time. I nearly died when I heard you went to the Harvard-Williams game. Pray tell who is Francis Biarley that he should be taking you to a game on such short acquaintance. It must be a sudden case. Bradford and HOWARD! in one day certainly is a lot for a little child like yourself.

Last Sunday night some of us went up to the Anderson's and we got our own supper. It was heaps of fun and the boys rough-housed perfectly awfully. A week from Sunday I think they are coming here for supper but I am not sure. Anyway they didn't act quite as badly as the boys did over at Helen's that night.

Please kick Betty Farrington and make her write to me.

OH SUGAR (that is the way I feel) Have you heard me speak about Leonard? Well anyway the boys down at school have started to tease him about me and the girls tease me about him. It is perfectly awful!! They write his name in my books and mine in his. We both have forth period vacant and so he comes and sits just behind me and when we start to whisper everybody giggles.

The only thing to do is to make a joke of it and so we have to laugh but it makes me so mad.

Leonard and Dorothy McGee were at Catherine Anderson's the other evening and they discussed me up and down. Catherine told me all about it afterwards. They started on my this-year's hat and then Leonard said he liked my last-year's one better. Then Leonard said he thought that I was about the nicest girl at Central this year. Ha! Ha! How's that for a little milk toast?

Well duty calls and I must go. Ta ta love

Your ownly[sic]

Cousin

P.S. Make Betty F write and please give my love to Clara [Turner] and her family, hum.

Last week I went to see "The Two Orphans" and yesterday I went to see "Caught in the Rain." They were both great.

Pen Hollowell is very sick and his mother has brought him home. Mother just told me. Isn't it awful?

Leila noted that while Betty attended school in Boston, she weekly visited the Turner house at 10 Francis Avenue in Cambridge. The Turners were Betty's sister Catharine's in-laws.

'Clara' was Epes Turner's sister. 'Howard,' who frequently escorted Betty on social occasions, was Clara and Epes' brother. Leila added, "He later became a professor of hydraulics at MIT."

Still Fall, 1910
Minneapolis, Minnesota

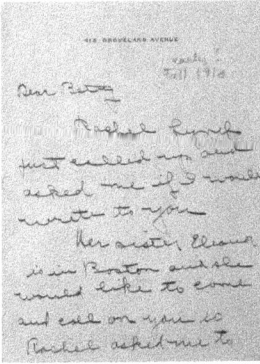

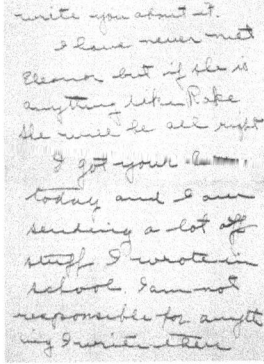

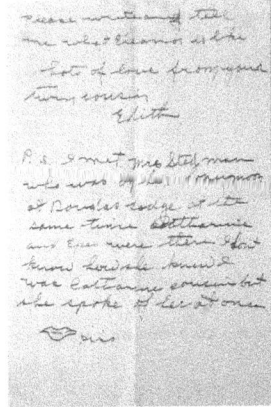

418 GROVELAND AVENUE

Dear Betty,

Rachel Lynch just called up and asked me if I would write to you.

Her sister Eleanor is in Boston and she would like to come and call on you so Rachel asked me to write you about it.

I have never met Eleanor but if she is anything like Rache she will be all right.

I got your letter today and I am sending a lot of stuff I wrote in school. I am not responsible for anything I write there. Please write and tell me what Eleanor is like.

Lots of love from your twin cousin
Edith

P.S. I met Mrs Stedman who was on her honeymoon at Douglas Lodge* at the same time Catharine** and Epes were there. I don't know how she knew I was Catharine's cousin but she spoke of her at once.
[Illustration of lips]
Kiss

---

*Douglas Lodge was described on the Internet as a "beautiful log cabin building in Itasca State Park about 100 miles northwest of Minneapolis." The star on the map shows its location by Minneapolis and Lake Superior.

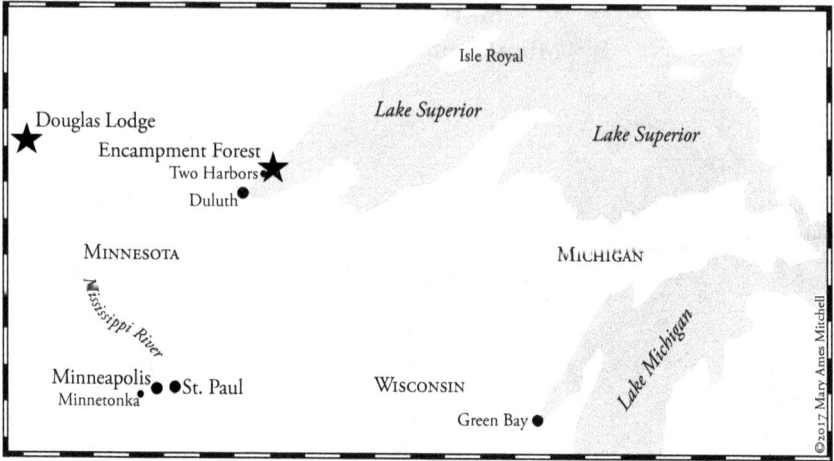

Isle Royal

Lake Superior

Lake Superior

Douglas Lodge

Encampment Forest
Two Harbors
Duluth

MINNESOTA

MICHIGAN

Mississippi River

Minneapolis
Minnetonka
St. Paul

WISCONSIN

Lake Michigan

Green Bay

©2017 Mary Ames Mitchell

*Catharine is Betty's older sister, the one who got married.

Still **Fall, 1910**
Minneapolis, Minnesota

418 GROVELAND AVENUE

Dear Betty,

I wrote you the other day but I don't know wether[sic] you got the letter or not because you haven't answered.

Monday night father went to Chicago and after he left, mother and I went to see "A Stranger in the Strange Land" at the Lyric. It was terribly funny. I have been to the Lyric every week since two weeks before the wedding and I am getting used to all the actors. They have a new leading man and he is a perfect peach. Then there is a man who is really only about eighteen years old. Even mother admits that.

Tell Betty Farrington I shall write as soon as I get a chance but I can't now because I have a Caesar test tomorrow and we are going out to dinner. Please give my love to her and a hug and kiss for you.

From your crazy cousin

October 26, 1910
Minnesota

Central High School
October 26th 1910

Dear Betty —

Please don't mind this paper because you will get it wether[sic] *you mind or not. Do tell me if you are seeing H O W A R D ! ! every week or not because if you are I shall commit suicide tonight as the clock strikes twelve.*

I suppose the same boy is taking you to all the Harvard games. You lucky enfant (Te He) notice the Francais. Ting! Ting! There goes the bell. Only five minutes more of fifteen minute period. I went to your house on Friday and stayed till Sunday after noon. Catharine is quite different [now that she is married] *and though it didn't seem possible she is about six times as darling as before.*

Sunday night four of us went to Dorothy McGee's to supper and I had the time of my life.

Last night Catherine Anderson, Margaret & Dorothy McGee, Leonard and Winthrop came over and we made candy. The fudge got all over the floor and the kitchen was a perfect fright when we finished but Florence [the Winter's cook] *is so good natured I don't think she will mind. I think your description of Mrs Bellow's sister is terribly funny and I am sure I should simply hate her.* [Mrs Bellow was Betty's landlady in Boston. She was a friend of Charles and Fanny Ames who, as mentioned, also lived in Boston.]

Next week we have no school on Thursday or Friday because of teachers meetings and I shall either (pronounced ī ther) go to St. Paul or the lake.

Yesterday our class had an Ancient History test and because I had an average of + + for the month I didn't have to take it. On my way back to my room I had to pass through Miss Forester's room and Raif Stevenson was having a class there. He thought I had been kicked out of class and simply hollered. I thought he would burst, he laughed so hard. Now I am trying to find him and explain.

Oh! did I tell you the news Lawrence Gregory and I are back on speaking terms and he about kills himself smiling when I meet him in the hall. As he sits in the next room and is in my English class that is quite often.

Betty darling I have a new case. He is the nicest thing imaginable and is quite good looking. Perhaps you met him up at dancing school, Selden Smith, but you wouldn't think much of him if you just met him. I didn't care a rap about him till the other day I got to talking to him at recess. Then I got it good and hard. We always wave at each other across the hall at recess and if we happen to meet each other we talk and I about die on the spot.

He lives down on Oak Grove and yesterday he walked home with a lot of other boys just ahead of me.

Every few minutes he would look around and I would become interested in the landscape. Then I could see the other boys laugh and punch him or tease him and they would almost have a scrape.

This morning he and another boy walked to school a couple of blocks behind me but I didn't dare turn around. You must think I am an idiot but remember yourself and Keith & Tom Daniels and Jimmy Haete[sp?] and all the others. Please don't say a word about all this to Betty Farrington because she just knew him at dancing school and probably doesn't care anything about him.

Now I have told you the whole thing but I wish I could see you because I could explain so much better.

Please write and say you don't think I am crazy.

From your twin

Edie

October 31, 1910
Minnesota

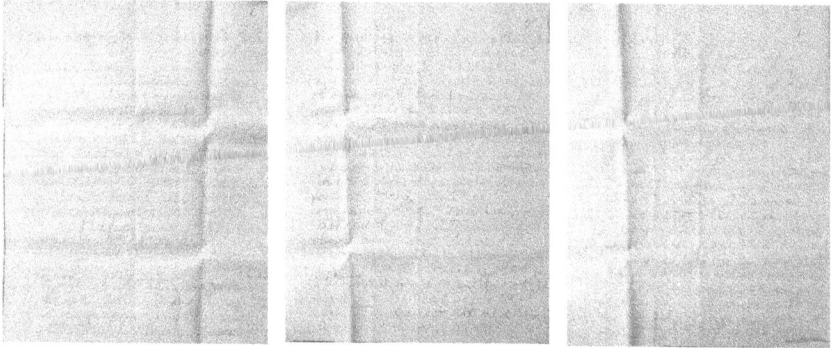

Central High
Monday
Oct 31st 1910

Dear Betty

I just stuck my finger in the ink so I am going to write with pencil.

I hope to goodness you didn't tell Betty F. about my last and worst because if you did I shall spread the good news about Keith all over Minneapolis. I shall rent space in the paper and put it where all may see, I shall shout it from the house tops so that all may hear and I shall write it in the peppermint oil that all may smell.

Disgusting word is smell but I can't say "All may odor." To-morrow I shall hie[sp?] me to the Russell coffee house and beg for sweet charities sake. In other words to-morrow (gee the five minute bell) is tag day. Friday in school Leonard came and sat behind me as he always does at fourth period. We talked so much that Mr. Lichl got mad and stopped his class and told Leonard to take a seat on the other side of the room. Every body turned and rubbered and I felt as if I cost 3 cents. At recess I could hear them way down the hall teasing poor Leonard.

There was a picture of me on the front page of the Sunday paper but Mother wouldn't let them put my name on it and nobody recognized it.

Oh heavens Leonard has come back to sit behind me again and I know Mr. Lichl is going to kick him out. —

A space of time has passed. I tried to do some Algebra for Leonard and couldn't do it. Lucky I don't have to do Freshman algebra again because I have forgotten the crazy stuff entirely.

Saturday night I had a Halloween party. Just five girls and five boys.

Some of them came to dinner and some came afterwards. I counted up afterwards and those that came to dinner were there four hours and a half from half past six to eleven.

While I am writing this I am trying to translate Caesar for a girl and she is explaining geometry to me so please don't mind if this outpouring from my soul is a little mixed. How I wish this period would endure forever because next comes recess and I must go and get my head taken off for not handing in a paper last Friday.

(Leonard is announcing that he is going to faint because he has solved a problem.)

Then Thursday and Friday of this week no school for me because there are teachers meetings and all the public schools get off.

Saturday night I am going to a play over at the University with Douglas*. Please tell me what fraternity do Jim and Don Catheorl[sp?] belong to.

Prehaps[sic] I shall go down to St Paul on Thursday and if I see any of the boys I shall say you send your love because I am sure you do.

Last Saturday I went to the Central North game and North beat 6 to 2. It was mostly because our boys have the big head and Rey fumbled forward passes. Central had not been scored on this year and we were so sure of the championship. Prehaps[sic] we'll get it if we beat West.

Lots of love

Edith

---

*'Douglas' was Thomas Winter's nephew from England. He was named after William Douglas, an important Winter ancestor who lived in Aberdeen in the 1600s. According to an interview by Lillian E. Taffe of Alice Ames Winter in the May 31, 1924, issue of *The Women's Citizen*, Alice and Tom "opened their home and undertook the task of parenting two children, a niece and nephew ... when the girl, Kittie Hubie, was twelve and the boy, Douglas Winter, was fourteen." Kittie eventually served as a trained nurse overseas during World War I. Before 1924, she married and moved to California. Douglas graduated from the University of Minnesota and, by 1924, served as a government inspector in agriculture in Minnesota. This was the only instance Edith mentioned either of them.

November 1, 1910
Minnesota

Central High School
Nov 1st 1910

Dear Betty,

Inclosed[sic] *please find one V.N. tag* in payment for which please send by return mail one kiss.*

[In the margin Edith wrote] *"I can't find tag, but send a kiss anyway.*

I hope you don't mind getting letters on school paper but I never get time to write outside of school.

About three days ago I got a great letter from Clara [Turner] *in which she said that you were out there almost every week. Lucky infant. I bet my last dollar you arrange it so that you are there at the same time that HOWARD is there. Do let me know if he is still as darling as ever. I am going to sell tags all afternoon so I really must get my lessons. I got my card today and these are my marks. – means failure, ± = just pass, + = good, ++ = excellent*

Caesar –
Geom +
Ancient History ++
English ++

Deportment ±

Past month I got
Caesor[sic] +
English ++
Ancient His ++
   Oh sugar

                         your lonely cousin
                              Edith

Do you remember that Miss Wilcox at the Lafayette hops who wore a black and white dress trimmed with red hobble skirt [who] *slapped boys faces? She is going to be at the same box as myself this afternoon.*

---

*I have yet to figure out what 'V.N. tags' were. Victory Now?

November 2, 1910
Minnesota

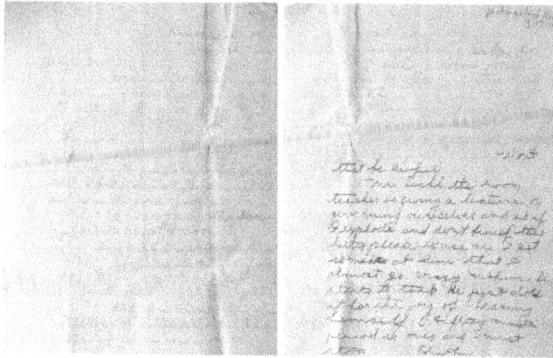

Central High School
November 2nd 1910

Dear Betty,

Again it is fifteen minute period and I am using it to write to you.

Yesterday was tag day and I sold tags from half past one to half past seven. We sold four hundred tags. That is including what the women who had our box in the morning sold and we got $119.59. Last year the same place only got $40.00.

We had a splendid time and after dinner we went to the lan? and watched them count.

Did you hear they are talking of uniting the two cities and naming them Minnehoha. Minne for Minneapolis and hoha for St Paul. Good joke Ha – Ha. Extremely rude.*

Tomorrow and Friday we have no school and I shall not see my angel boy for four days. Won't that be awful.

Mr. Lichl the room teacher is giving a lecture on governing ourselves and so if I explode and don't finish this letter please excuse me. I get so mad at him that I almost go crazy when he starts to talk. He just does it for the joy of hearing himself. Fifteen minute period is over and I must stop.

Edith

---

*Leila commented, 'Minnehoha' is still a standard put down of St. Paul."

November 10, 1910
Minnesota

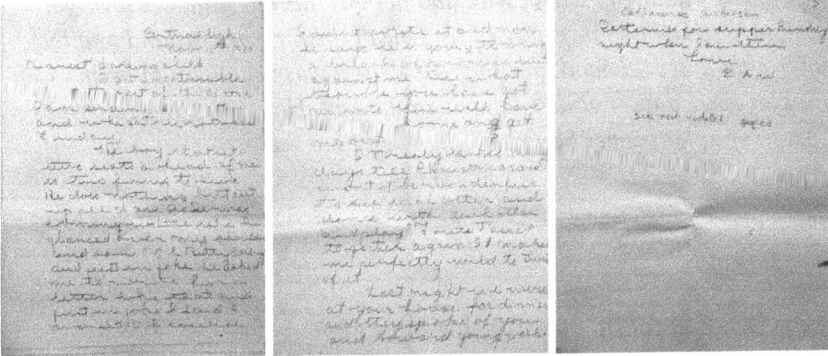

Central High School
November 10th 1910

Dearest darling child

I got into trouble about the rest of the letter I am sending with this and which I wrote last Friday.

The boy that sits two seats ahead of me is too funny to live. He does nothing but cut up all day. As he was coming up the [a]isle he glanced over my shoulder and saw "Oh Betty darling" and just in joke he asked me to write him a letter like that and just in joke I said I would. Of course I didn't write it and now he says he is going to bring a breach of promise suite against me. See what trouble you have got me into. You will have to come home and get me out.

It really isn't so many days till Christmas and won't it be wonderful to see each other and dance with each other and play "Toute Passe" to-gether again. It makes me perfectly wild to think of it.

Last night we were at your house for dinner and they spoke of you and Howard going walking together and Epes said Howard enjoyed it so much. I was crazy to tell them what you thought on the subject but I restrained myself.

I don't know my geometry and I don't know my English but I don't care a rap when I look at those bridesmaid pictures and see that picture of Howard. I almost pack up and go east. By the way do you write to either Tom or Keith? Remember to answer this question in your next letter. I saw that Mr. and Mrs. Daniels were going to be at the "St. Paul"* [Hotel] for the winter, quite spiffy are they not. Every body who sees those bridesmaids *pictures falls desperately in love with you so you will have quite a crowd of people crazy about you when you come home. Really I am getting awfully jealous.*

I was walking to school with another girl this morning when we got almost to school two boys passed us. One of them turned around and took off his hat and said good morning. My dear it was Seldon and I hadn't seen him for three days. I almost fainted on the spot. He is going to Catherine's [Anderson] *for supper Sunday night when I am there.*

Love

E. A. W.

---

*Leila said that the St. Paul Hotel is still spiffy.

November 1910
Minnesota

This undated letter was in the same envelope as the November 10th letter above.

Central High School
Dearest Elizabeth,
Here it is fifteen minute period again and so I suppose I must write to you. Don't you wish you were at home because I am going to have a houseparty at the lake this week end. And Seldon Smith is coming. At least I hope so because I am going to ask him.
Last night we were at Catherine Anderson's for supper and he was there. I never got into such a rough-house in my life. I got flour all through my hair and all over my face till I looked like a scare-crow. We had such a funny supper. First Winthrop made some stuff he called "Cheese dreams"/ nightmares all right, and then we ate them before they got cold. Then we started stuff on the chafing-dish and while that was cooking we ate our desert and cake.
Catherine and I had great big frilly aprons and the boys wore great big kitchen aprons and they did look so funny. Well goodbye my lady love. Farewell my turtle dove. You are the only (only nit) Please write me about the boys next door.
<u>*Tuesday*</u>
On Saturday you of course will wear crimson [Harvard's school color] and please think of me telephoning every two minutes to find out the score. Please let me know right away if you are going to wear an American Beauty

[rose] *or just a red rose. I think the plain roses match our ribbons better.*

Oh Betty, Harvard has just got to win. Central has got the championship of North Dakota and Friday we play for the championship here. Do hope and pray for us because we need it. Yesterday I heard "Toute Passe" played for the first time since you left and it made me want to scream. Please excuse the envelope I send this in but I can't find any other to fit the paper.

Love Edith.

November 11, 1910
Minnesota

This letter ends abruptly with no signature. The final pages must be lost or mis-filed.

Central High School
November 11th 1910

Dearest Betty,
Yesterday afternoon I went to the Orpheum. The first thing were
"Representative ballads of Sweden." They were awfully good and rather
uncommon. Then the Milch sisters* appeared. First elder Milch sang an
awfully pretty song, then younger Milch played a rotton[sic] violin solo.
Then she accompanied elder Milch in another song.
Next came a terribly funny skit. The scene was the wall of a baseball
field with dirty papers, tin cans and a messenger and a little girl peaking
through the fence. The little girl was terribly funny. Her knees were coming
through her stockings and her dress was in shreds. They hollered and
screeched for their team. Then an Englishman came on. He used long, long
words and the girl would faint onto the boy and they would go on a heap in
the floor or she would ly[sic] down on her face and kick the air. They had
quite a long skit that was awfully funny.
There were two men who had a skit called "Breaking into Vaudeville."
They sang. "Plunk Phink sang the little Mr Bullfrog" then they sang a song
in which the chorus began "Splash! that was Galiger" and ended with "Oh-
you can't keep the Irish down." Another went
(Harry) "My wife's away"

(George) Why then
(Harry) I'm free
(both) Hurrah for summertime.
The audience applauded and applauded so they walked across the stage sing[ing] *(without looking at audience) "It's a terrible death to die. It's a terrible death to die."*

---

*Leila added, "The Milch Sisters entertained regularly at one of the hotels in Minneapolis during the 1920s and 1930s. They sang light, classical, tearoom music."

November 17, 1910
Minnesota

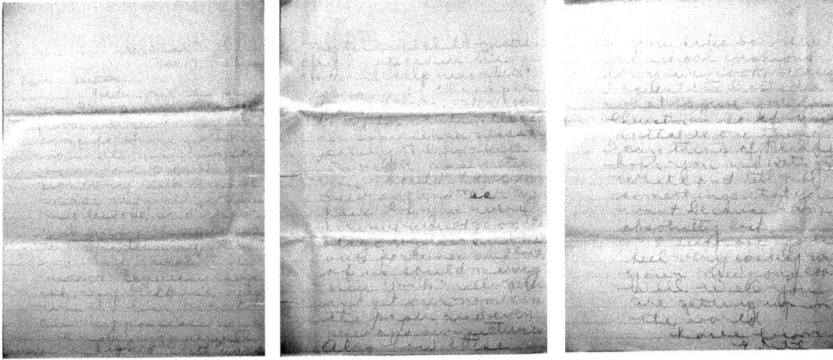

Central High
Nov 17th 1910

Dear Betty
      Hear my last prayer. I am going into battle from which I may never come forth. In other words the next two periods I have English and Geometery[sic] tests. I have made my will (studied my lessons) and I leave you every thing except my bridesmaid dress in which I wish to be buried. Especially cherish my black ear-rings which I love above all my possessions.
      Enough. Farewell.
      Signed Edith Ames Winter

My beloved child, yesterday I noticed in the "female help wanted" column of the paper this ad. "Wanted, a young lady for vaudeville act no experience necessary, salary to begin with 15 a week apply etc." You should have seen me rant and tear my hair. If you were here we would go on the stage together and make our fortunes and both of us could marry New York millionaires and get our names in the paper and even prehaps[sic] our pictures. Alas how these chances do slip by.
      Seldon walked to school with me again this morning. Oh joy I saw him about a block behind me when I turned down Nicollet [a major avenue in Minneapolis] and he ran and caught up with me. Sunday evening Leonard and I had a scrape and we hadn't spoken all week but he spoke today so it is all right. I am absolutely sure that I am going to flunk in Geometry so please symaphies[sic] with me.
      I have started on my Christmas presents and last night I finished a

pink satin opera glass bag lined with white satin. If I say it as shouldn't I think it is one of the prettyes[sic] opera glass bags I have ever seen.

Betty Farrington writes that you carry on something fierce with the boys next door. Will I be surprised and shocked when I think of poor Tom [Daniels] working away at Yale or Jail or the workhouse. Just as you say.

Do you like banners and school cushions for your room because I haven't the least idea what to give you for Christmas so if you do that is one thing I can think of. Please both you and Betty F. write and tell me somethings that you want because I am absolutely lost.

I suppose you feel very cocky with your new pony coat. Well Well you are getting up in the world.

Love from
Edith

December 2, 1910
Minnesota

Central High
Dec 2nd 1910

Dearest Betty,

I don't remember when I sent my last letter so you may have some very stail[sic] news. Last Monday was Mother's birthday and we went to see "The Chocolate Soldier" at the Lyric. It was perfectly wonderful and the man that played the chocolate soldier was too good looking for words. I have been going around ever since humming "Come come I love you only" and "For I'm a chocolate soldier man." Tuesday I went to a tea for Mary Louise Edsall*, Harmon's sister. She came out this year and is engaged to a Mr. Harrington (I think that's his name) in the east. I spent Tuesday night at the Anderson's and two of the boys came over. Wednesday I had my millinery lesson. Yesterday for certain reasons (ahem) mother made me stay in the house. Tonight I am going to a dancing school party with Winthrop and every other Friday night I am to go to the dancing school with Seldon. Saturday afternoon I hope to go to the Lyric and in the evening I am going to some performance at the Radisson. Sunday I am going to supper at Dorothy McGee's and next week I don't know what I am going to do. This afternoon I am going down to the Auditorium to see the decorations for the Hostesses which is tonight. That is all I can think of and there goes the bell for Latin.

Love from
Edith

---

*I received an email from Jonathan K.M. Edsall, the grandson of Harmon Edsall mentioned above. Jon stated that his great-aunt, "Mary Louise Edsall, married Ferris Sands Hetherington on December 31, 1911." That would have been just over a year after my grandmother wrote this letter.

April 15, 1912

Julia Frances 'Fanny' (Baker) Ames and Charles Gordon Ames (c.1900)

During the time between Edith's last letter and her next letter, Betty and Edith's mutual grandfather — the man who links the cousins pulling this book together — Charles Gordon Ames, passed away in Boston. He was eighty-four years old. I have numerous photos of him. One is encased in a frame that my father said 'CGA' carved himself. I have three additional pieces of CGA memorabilia: his desk and two books he wrote. *A Book of Prayers* by Charles Gordon Ames was published by the American Unitarian Association in Boston in 1908. *Charles Gordon Ames: A Spiritual Autobiography with an epilogue by Alice Ames Winter* was published by Houghton Mifflin Company in Boston in 1913.

I have read a few of the prayers and the entire autobiography. In the latter, my great-great-grandfather described entering Geauga Seminary in Chester Cross Roads outside Cleveland in 1847 to become a Free Baptist minister. In 1850, he was sent to save souls in The Frontier. He married his first wife, Sarah Daniels, Betty's grandmother, that year in New Hampshire. They eventually moved to St. Anthony Falls [later Minneapolis] when "all the territory of Minnesota could hardly have contained more than six thousand white settlers, as well as the Sioux Indians. ...

"The settlers were mostly from Maine and saluted each other as 'Maniacs.' There were Irish and half-breed French; the Roman Church was in the lead; four Protestant sects had made a beginning; the people were taxing themselves on true New England principles to establish the library and the school. ... By 1853 the land on the west side of the Mississippi had been opened to settlement, and many thousands of people from many states were making clearings, building shanties and starting farms, building mills and laying out town sites for purposes of speculation. Minneapolis was just coming into existence." Charles and Sarah were among those thousands.

Sarah Jane (Daniels), adopted daughter Serena Marie, Charles Wilberforce and Charles Gordon Ames c.1860.
Tin plate housed in the Massachusetts Historical Society.

Charles wrote, "The Free-Will Baptists had taught me to be an ardent opponent of slavery as well as of intemperance, and in a small way I became an agitator. In 1854, I was the secretary of a convention called to protest against the passage of the Kansas and Nebraska Bill, which threw open the new territories to slavery."

Through his friendship with John Wessley North, who President Lincoln later appointed as a judge of the supreme court of Nevada Territory, Charles began to reconsider his religious views.

"Whatever I read or heard seemed to suggest larger interpretations of the universe [than the] doctrine of eternal punishment."

Doubts led to a "theological crisis." "I soon found myself like a lad who still wears the garments he is outgrowing, and who feels himself at once pinched and half covered. Still living inside these earlier notions, my mind was rapidly expanding beyond them in all directions. ... One of my serious problems was how to account for goodness outside of the churches. ... There awoke a passionate desire for a more inclusive fellowship, for a Church broad enough to hold all faithful people, or certainly all true Christians. ... I was gradually finding out that much of the beautiful morality of the Bible belonged to other ancient writings and was shared by the better sort of pagans. ... In solitary hours I held serious dialogue with myself. ... In May, 1856, I withdrew from the Free Baptist Church in Minneapolis, which I had organized nearly five years before. In July, 1859, I wrote my name as a member of the church of the Disciples in Boston, little thinking that thirty years later I should be there as its pastor."

Charles described many more adventures along the way. At the end of the Civil War – for which he paid someone to take his place in the Union Army so he could continue as a preacher - he traveled to California via the isthmus, followed a year and a half later by his second wife, Fanny, and their baby daughter, Alice. Many years later, in the Epilogue to Charles' autobiography, Alice described how her father preached first on Sundays in Santa Cruz. Then, in a horse-drawn cart, he "climbed the twisting roads to San José where another congregation gathered. ... Everywhere where two or three could be gathered together, to Watsonville, Santa Clara, Sacramento, the missionary zeal carried him."

While in California, Fanny gave birth to a son, Theodore, "the child with the glowing eyes of the Sistine baby, whose brief life left an exquisitely sensitive spot in the family consciousness, like a wonderful promise unfulfilled," wrote Alice. Her own son, Gilbert, would leave that same promise for her, Tom and Edith many years later. Charles returned his family east to Germantown, Pennsylvania, in 1872.

In 1884, Charles spoke alongside Susan B. Anthony and other

civil rights leaders at the fiftieth anniversary of the organization of the American Anti-Slavery Society.

Reading CGA's autobiography was one of the things that inspired me to unearth my family's history and bring it back to the light. I hope my children will experience the thrill from hearing these stories that I do. An entire book could be written about CGA's support of abolition and women's rights. His daughter Alice carried on his legacy, whereas his granddaughter Edith did not.

The family tree below shows Charles Gordon Ames' children and grandchildren from his two wives, Sarah Jane Daniels and Fanny Baker.

[Partial list]
Descendants of the Rev. Charles Gordon Ames (1828-1912)

m#1 on 28 Mar 1850
Sarah Jane Daniels (1828-1861)

Charles 'Willie' 'Charley' Wilberforce Ames (1855-1921)
m. 1883 **Mary Inches Lesley** (1854-1929) d/o **Professor J. Peter Lesley** (1819-1903) & **Susan Inches Lyman** (1823-1904)

Adopted **Serena Miriam Huntley** (1840-?) Took the name **Serena Marie Ames**

Charles 'Les' Lesley Ames (1884-1969)
m. 1917 **Linda Worthington Baker** (1893-1985)

Margaret Ames* (1885-1956)
m. 1917 **Cushing Frederick Wright** (1879-1971)

Catharine Ames* (1887-1947) m. 24 Sep 1910 **Samuel 'Epes' Turner, III** (1884-1945)

Alice Ames* (1889-1976) m. 1916 **Bronson Crothers M.D.** (1854-1959)

Elizabeth 'Betty' Ames (12 Aug 1894-5 Mar 1990) m.1922 **Norris Dean Jackson** (1895-29 Sep 1990)

Theodore Gordon Ames* (1898-1969) m. 1927 **Barbara 'Bee' Holt** (1905-1998)

Mary Lesley Ames (1923-present) m#1 **William Andrews**, m#2 **Edwin Wolff**

Sarah 'Sally' Ames* (1925-present) m#1 **Francis Ellis**, m#2 **Adam Yarmolinsky**

Leila Dean Jackson* (1924-present) m. **Leon Poullada**

Catharine 'Kitty' Ames* Jackson (1926-present) m. 1952 **Sergeant 'Sarge' Woodhull Wise**

[**Charles Morrison**] British, lived w/family during WWII (1929-2016)

m#2 on 25 Jun 1863
Julia Frances 'Fanny' Baker (1840-1931)

Lillian Ames (1864-1864) d. age 6 mo.

Alice Vivian Ames (1865-1944) m. 25 Jun 1892 **Thomas Gerald Winter** (1864-1934)

Theodore Ames (1870-1871) d. age 1yr 3mo.

Edith 'Aunt E' Theodora Ames (1874-1964) m. 25 Jun 1900 **Raymond Moreau Crosby** (1874/6-1945)

Charles Gilbert Winter (1893-1907) d. age 14

Edith Ames Winter (1895-1965) m. 27 Jun 1919 **Knowlton Lyman Ames, Jr. 'Juny' 'Snake'** (1893-1965) m#2 **Paul McGinnis** (1896-1965)

Knowlton 'Bud' Lyman Ames III (1920-2001) m. 21 Jun 1947 **Jayne Rubicam Skirm**

Thomas 'Tom' Winter Ames (1922-1970) m. 21 Jul 1950 **Eileen Mary 'Betty May' Hopkins**

Robert 'Bob' Dawes Ames (1925-2009) m. 23 Nov 1945 **Kathryn 'Kay'Ann Wallace**

* Has descendants not mentioned in this volume.

Among the family papers that Betty saved in the attics and closets of 501 Grand now housed in the Schlesinger Library were some poems and a short autobiography written by Charles Gordon's youngest daughter, Edith Theodora Ames. Edith Theodora was Edith Winter's aunt, Betty Ames' half-aunt, and Alice Ames Winter's only living sibling. Edith and Betty referred to her as 'Aunt E.' Edith Winter was named after her, and I was named after Edith Winter. Among Betty's files is a book of poetry Edith Theodora wrote as well as a poem that honored her father on what would have been his eighty-fifth birthday on October 3, 1913.

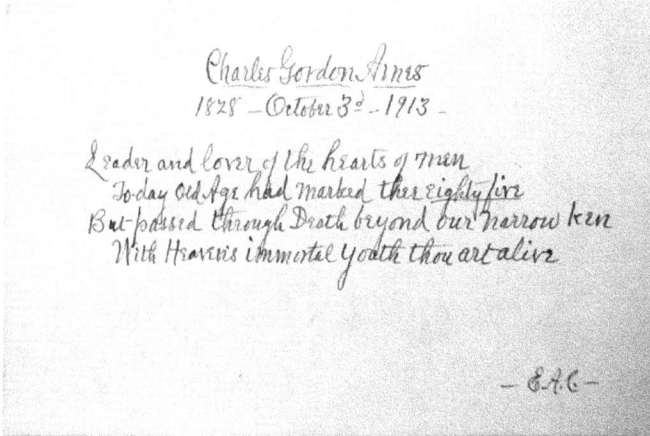

Charles Gordon Ames
1828 — October 3rd — 1913
Leader and lover of the hearts of men
Today Old Age had marked thee eighty-five
But-passed through Death beyond our narrow ken
With Heaven's immortal youth thou art alive

—E.A.C—

Twelve years before CGA's death, in 1900, when Edith Winter was five and Betty six, their Aunt E married Yale graduate Raymond Moreau Crosby, a successful illustrator. "His illustrations had been in demand by major magazines since the 1880s," wrote Leila. In 1905, Crosby illustrated a novel that his sister-in-law, Alice, wrote: *The Prize to the Hardy*. It was about a young débutante growing up in Minneapolis in the early 1900s. The woman's father, a grain merchant like Alice's husband, Tom (Edith's father), had migrated west from New England. Her mother was a native American Indian. Inter-racial marriage was a touchy subject at the time of Alice's writing. The débutante struggled choosing a husband among suitors who spouted a variety of 'isms,' such as communism, socialism, and futurism. Alice wrote a sequel called *Jewel Weed* in 1906, illustrated by Harrison Fisher.

At the time of CGA's death, Edith Theodora was thirty-eight years old and working as a costume designer. "She was very like her father in face and temperament," wrote Leila, her great-niece.

Aunt E and Raymond, who is drawing on a paper cup.

I found the above examples on AmericanArtArchives.com. Crosby drew the illustration on the left for the Red Cross in 1918. He drew the other two illustrations for *Life* magazine, one in 1919 and the other in 1924.

Getting back to the time period of Edith's letters, in 1913 Betty graduated from Miss Winsor's School in Boston and left for Italy. Between 1913 and 1914, she studied French, Italian and Art History with sixteen other young women at the Nixon Sheldon School in Fiesole near Florence. The Internet article below by Honor Moore includes a description of the school and helps us imagine Betty's experience. Ms. Moore had written a book about her grandmother, the painter Margaret Sargent, who attended the Nixon School "with other society graduates of Miss Porters School."*

Moore wrote, "The Florentine School, run by an American, Miss Nixon, mainly for American girls, was one of three finishing schools in Florence in 1910. [That year] thirteen girls inhabited the towered ivy-clad villa Nixon leased on the Via Barbacane, a narrow street that led up steeply from the square in San Gervasio, a village near San Domenico in the hills below Fiesole, about thirty minutes from the center of the city.

"When Miss Nixon's students took the tram down the hill for pastries, a teacher went along. Miss Nixon feared the young men who loitered on Via Tornabuoni near Doney's – titled young Florentines without a cent, who, in search of an American wife, routinely questioned the concierges of the Excelsior and the Grand Hotel about lineages of young American female guests; if she wasn't rich, they weren't interested. As an antidote, Miss Nixon invited American, English and Italian young men of whom she approved for thés dansants [tea dances].

"Miss Nixon's intention was that a young girl's year at the Florentine School familiarize her with the great sights of Italy. [She] took them to such places as Pompeii and the Riviera. ... The students referred to her as 'the chaperon of the Florentine School.'"

Betty's daughter Kitty wrote, "Mummy had a marvelous time in Fiosole and we children grew up listening to passionate stories about it and were infected with a love of Italy and France."

Betty Ames' studies were interrupted on July 28, 1914, when a young man from Serbia sparked the first world war by killing Archduke Franz Ferdinand of Austria. As Italy allied with England and France against Germany, Austria and Hungary, Betty returned to St. Paul.

Edith and Betty's families soon involved themselves in America's effort to help the French after the allies chased the Germans out of their country. On their way out, the Germans had grabbed every able-bodied

French man, woman and child capable of working in a factory, in the trenches, or in agriculture, and taken them back to Germany. They stole the remaining food. They destroyed farms and farming equipment. They burned villages, leaving behind small helpless children, wounded soldiers, and the aged – most of them sick, infested with lice, homeless and hungry. Many people, including hundreds of children, suffered from the effects of being gassed. [We will talk more about the gassing later.]

Betty's family joined the American Fund for French Wounded [A.F.F.W.] originally founded by women in New York to help the impoverished French. Betty's mother, listed as Mrs. C.W. Ames, chaired the St. Paul Minneapolis committee.

Edith's father was an official with the Red Cross. The two groups combined efforts.

The following description of Charles Wilberforce's war efforts was written by Arthur Sweeney** of St. Paul, Minnesota.

"Early in the war Charles Wilberforce Ames perfected an organization for the French war sufferers; he made a visit to France in 1916 to confer with those who were administering relief to the suffering; and he contributed a [hospital supply truck] to the cause. He converted his home into a workshop in which his family and friends labored unceasingly in providing bandages, clothing, and other necessities to bring relief to the destitute of the warring countries. His contribution of material as well as of money to this work was very large."

The A.F.F.W. asked for donations of $4,000 each to establish dispensaries in the French countryside. The amount "guaranteed the proper maintenance, medicines, rent, lights, initial equipment of instruments, tables, basins, running water, heat, etc. for a year at least."

Charles W. was one of the first to make such a donation. When he traveled to Paris to help deliver the donations to the hospitals, he took Betty's sisters Margaret and Alice and their brother Teddy with him. Betty stayed behind to help her mother with the Fund's activities in their home in St. Paul. One big job was assembling 'comfort sacks', also known as 'surprise bags,' for the service men. Each was filled with donations from the community. Hand knitted socks were a favorite.

A report for the Red Cross*** described how the donations were received on the 'front.'

"It is a little surprising to find a Major General taking the trouble to distribute the contents of a few bails and cases, but the fact proves how highly warm things are valued at the front and above all that the A.F.F.W. holds a special place in the sentiment and affection of the French army.

To them it is a bit of the U.S.A. they have visited and known; that they care for and that has cared for them. A regular ceremony has been made of the arrival of some dozens of our sweaters and socks. It is flattering but it is more than that; it is a gesture of real fraternity and appreciation of which we are justly proud.

"And you workers at home, who are inclined to feel that knitting sweaters is dull work, who have made so many socks that you do it mechanically now without thinking of the men who are to wear them, who are even beginning to wonder if it is worth while and if one pair more or less can make any difference; just try to imagine for a minute how cold it is in a Poste de Secours and then picture your socks being distributed by a Major General."

Meanwhile, in September of 1916, we find Edith on a train heading off to her sophomore year at Wellesley College in Massachusetts.

———————

*Moore, Honor. *The White Blackbird: A life of the painter Margaret Sargent* by her granddaughter, Viking Press, New York, 1996/2009

**Obituary of Charles Wilberforce Ames by Arthur Sweeney: https://archive.org/stream/jstor-20160382/20160382_djvu.txt

***"American Fund for French Wounded" *Monthly Report*, Vol. II. Sep-Oct 1917, Library Filing Number D 629.F8 08, Metal Edge, Inc. 2007 https://archive.org/stream/americanfundforf00newy/americanfundforf00newy_djvu.txt.]

Sketch of Tower Court built between 1914 and 1916. Source: New England Magazine, *October 1914, https://wellesleyhistory.wordpress.com/page/2*

Wellesley

⸺◈⸺

According to the "Wellesley History" website, Edith's home during college, Tower Court, was built after a massive fire on March 17, 1914, destroyed Wellesley's principal building, College Hall. "Hours after the fire, as the ruins of College Hall lay smoldering, the school closed and the students were sent home, nearly 500 of them taking the 6:04 Boston Express to Grand Central Station in New York City. When they returned three weeks later, a temporary wooden building (known as the 'Hen-Coop' because of its appearance) had been constructed at the base of the hill which College Hall had sat upon. Although the Hen-Coop provided space for classes and administrative offices, finding rooms for the students to live in was a more difficult matter. Fortunately, many girls who lived in the other dormitories were more than willing to share their rooms with their displaced classmates. Almost immediately, the institution began an ambitious fundraising campaign in order to rebuild its campus ... it raised over two million dollars ($750,000 ... from the Rockefeller Foundation). By the fall of 1915... Tower Court had been built on the site of College Hall."

September 24, 1916
Massachusetts

EAW

Dearest Elizabeth:–

It is 3 p.m. September 24th and I am busily occupied in thinking of you and Catharine and Epes, of five years and three small children: However I find myself totally unable to write a poem, or even an essay on the subject so what shall I sing. There isn't a soul I know on this fool train and the only encouraging looking people are two lads wearing unknown hatbands who are traveling with a girl to whom one of them is married (very recently). Where the other man comes in I can't say. My ink gave out on the train so I am now finishing this letter at dear old Wellesley.

My room here is absolutely palatial – and completely furnished in gray furniture which matches the gray madras cloth on the walls and the grey woodwork. A full length mirror is set into the door of the enormous closet and there is a long window seat which opens and holds all my linen under the double casement window with leaded glass panes.

Tower Court isn't finished yet downstairs. We are to have our meals at Stone Hall for a few weeks and they say the living rooms won't be ready until Christmas and the elevators aren't working yet, but it is going to be beautiful when it is done and the comfort of the upstairs more than compensates for any other inconvenience.

And the girls are adorable! All my particular crowd are living here and we have been simply hanging around each other's rooms every minute of the time. Then right after supper last night Avouelle came up and she is dearer than ever, if possible. We talked and talked and then went down to the Christian Association reception for the freshmen and I introduced her to everybody as my freshman and then we went to the vill[age] and I bought a waste basket and some bread and jam for our gang breakfast this morning and then we went to the drugstore and consumed ice-cream after which she walked half way home with me. You know she is a member of the faculty now; assisting Miss Bates in the Lit department and she has the most adorable little suite down at the hotel.

Before I went to bed last night I was all unpacked except for my dresses which I am leaving in my trunk until I get some hangers to put them on.

A young mob breakfasted in my room and now another mob has assembled and begun another breakfast and I am writing my belovedest cousin because I am very fond of her and I hope she will answer it.

My guests however, seem to look to me for entertainment – so goodbye dear.

Thine
Otto.

Postmarked **September 30, 1916**
Wellesley College, Massachusetts

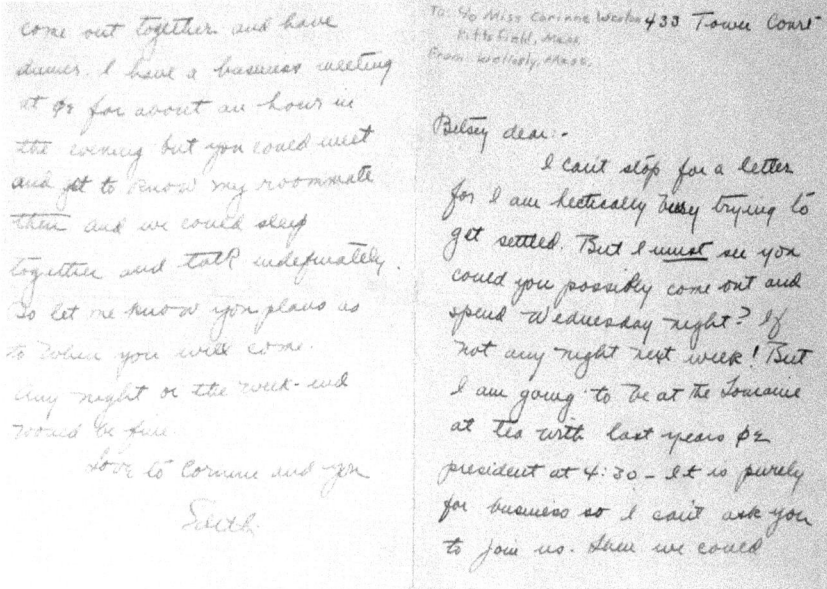

Edith begins to address Elizabeth as 'Betsy,' a nickname that Betty's
daughter Leila said no one else in her family ever used.

——————————

Envelope:
Miss Elizabeth Ames
c/o Miss Corinne Weston [who became a lifelong friend of Betty's]
Pittsfield, Mass.

Letter:

433 Tower Court

Betsy dear:–
        *I can't stop for a letter for I am hectically busy trying to get settled. But
I must see you. Could you possibly come out and spend Wednesday night?
If not any night next week! But I am going to be at the Touraine* [a shop
on Central Street] at tea with last years ΦΣ president at 4:30 – It is purely
for business so I can't ask you to join us. Then we could come out together
and have dinner. I have a business meeting at ΦΣ for about an hour in the*

evening but you could meet and get to know my roommate then and we could sleep together and talk indefinitely. Do let me know your plans as to when you will come.

Any night or the weekend-end would be fine.

Love to Corinne and you

Edith.

---

*La Touraine refers to the elegant chateaux region in west-central France.

October 15, 1916
Wellesley College, Massachusetts

Tower Court
Station B
October 15 [1916]

Dearest Betsy: —
Why don't you write, I am so deserted and forlorn that it is tragic – Yes I know the life of a settlement worker is a busy one, but — well dear, I have averaged about 6½ hours sleep a night for the last week so you can see I am busy too. Last Monday the society announcements came out and I got Phi Sigma, my first choice and the best part of it is that most of my friends are to be there with me, and Avouelle is my sponsor. So I am dreadfully happy — Initiations are tomorrow, preceded by hair washing, bath, all white clothes and a dinner at the Inn. ΦΣ is really going to mean a lot and I am too pleased about it to move. Then too we are in the throes of a class struggle. We are trying to elect a Junior president and we balloted from 4:30 to 7 last night, adjourned the meeting till 8 this morning, balloted for half an hour and suspended operations till noon without being able to obtain a majority on any of our three candidates. Behold a grand mess!
Then too there is Junior Play work, consultations, and pursuing after elusive authorities. And study — oh Lord, these guys have no mercy!
Continued Sunday
Initiations are over – very quiet and impressive and also we have elected our president – a peach, good friend of mine and a ΦΣ – isn't that great.

This morning we all had breakfast down at the house and fooled around down there till 11. My official job, inherited from my sponsor, and her sponsor before her, is to look after the garbage and keep the chute clean. And all my friends are convulsed and joyful. You know I can't convince anybody there that I know a broom from a duster or that I have ever had my hands in dish water. They refuse to believe in my plebeian home surroundings – But I will show them.

When you come east I will have to have a party or a tea for you there, it is so wonderful to have a nice homelike place to take people to.

Please take a minute from the unregenerate Irish [charities] and write me a note now and then because, for some strange rfeason I am fond of you.

Shine
Otto

Postmarked **November 6, 1916**
Wellesley, Massachusetts

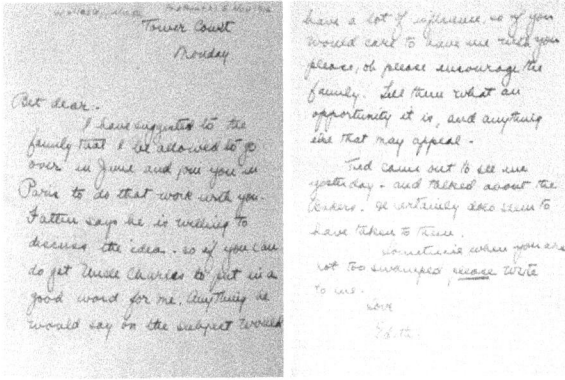

'Uncle Charles' is Betty's father and 'Ted' is Theodore. Betty thought she would leave for France earlier than she did.

———

Tower Court
Monday

Bet dear: —
    I have suggested to the family that I be allowed to go over in June and join you in Paris to do that work with you. Father says he is willing to discuss the idea. So if you can, do get Uncle Charles to put in a good word for me. Anything he would say on the subject would have a lot of influence – so if you would care to have me with you please, oh please encourage the family. Tell them what an opportunity it is, and anything else that may appeal.
    Ted came out to see me yesterday – and talked about the Bakers. He certainly does seem to have taken to them.
    Sometime when you are not too swamped please write to me.
                Love,
                Edith

Probably **1916**
Wellesley College

Tower Court
Thursday

Betsy dear:

Where are you? It is too long since I have heard from you that it seems almost as if you were a stranger. But then, when anything particular happens I always come back to you for sympathy. So open your ears and prepare to apprehend.

Well, the house-party was wonderful. We danced more than I ever expected to this side of heaven and Sunday night we went on a sleigh ride up into Vermont for supper and then began dancing at twelve and danced till time to rush for our 4.a.m train from North Adams. Richie was sweet, and most tactful for he gave me every possible opportunity to play with Ruf.* But somehow I didn't get on so well with the dear man and I left Williamstown feeling that I had my sanity quite within my grasp again.

But last Sunday night, when two Williams men who were at the houseparty were out here playing with Dee and myself, Ruf called up and asked if he might come down for Washington's birthday. Ellen Stetson's grandfather has just died so the party there was off and I said I would be pleased to see his sweet face again. Meanwhile Maynard asked me to a dance that day and threw fits both over the phone and by letter when he heard the news.

Well I certainly am glad George W. was born, for I did enjoy his birthday. I went in about noon and Ruf got a big car and we went for a drive. When we got back to the Copley [a fashionable hotel in Boston] a delicious luncheon which he had ordered was waiting and after that we *bounced into a taxi and rolled off to see "It Pays to Advertise" and laughed ourselves sick. Then back to the Copley for tea, and I caught the last allowable train back to Wellesley. He was supposed to go back to Williams that night but he had told the dean some fearful tale before he came down so when he telegraphed "I find I can see her on Wednesday. Will you make it possible for me to stay over" the dean telegraphed back that he would make it possible and on Wednesday morning I was surprised with a night letter and a telephone call and so I dashed off to town again and went to the theater and then danced till time for the last train. After that the dear man did go back, at least I have heard nothing from him today – and all day I have been wandering about like a lost woman.*

By the way I have a terrific cold and I am supposed to be ill. Ruf recommends a little two sum[sic] trip to Hot Springs. Whew! Well, now that I have the whole tale off my shoulders to you I feel better, and we can revere (ō something else. Oh yes, while still on the subject, Maynard is still with us. I am going to the theater and thé dasant at the Copley on Saturday.)

Well then! Marks[grades] came out today and I got off better than ever before, so I feel that my neglect of the academic this past semester has been justifiable. I do so love to get good marks without really working for them.

I have seen lots of people both of us know lately – Grace Warner* is always at the thé dasants at the Copley and she was up at Williamstown too, as were Betty Farrington and Kitty McCahill and then I saw Xandra Robertson** across the room but not to speak to. Then Ted Brown was at the same houseparty we were – the poor man is desperately and hopelessly in love with a Providence girl. I sort of have an atmosphere of being at home which is very pleasant.

Oh Bet dear, why aren't you here to spend tonight with me. It would be so wonderful to have you to talk to. But you absolutely must write to me. And tell me the news. I haven't heard a peep from St Paul for ages and ages –

Same, as ever

Otto.

---

*Betty's niece, Mary Wolff, identified 'Ruf' as Rufus Rand of Minneapolis. His mother was in the Women's Club of Minneapolis with Alice Winter. 'Ted' is Ted Brown of St Paul. The 'Providence girl' is Phyllis Perrin, who Ted Brown later married.

**Leila said that Xandra Robertson later became Mrs. Arnold Kalman.

Probably **1916**
Wellesley College

History Class
Saturday

Dear Bet: –

I am so glad that you really will come out – either Monday or Tuesday would be good for me – I will enclose a time table in this and you let me know what day and what train you will come on and I will be beaming on the platform. Your letter was brought me in class and I will take this to the village directly after class, get an envelope, and mail it to thee.

I am going to be at Tower Court at one to 2 tomorrow, and probably from eight to 10, the telephone is Wellesley 1097. Oh, you will have to ask the operator for the Tower Court telephone number, or if you would mail me a special delivery this afternoon it would come to cheer me on the Sabbath. I am afraid I couldn't meet any train from 4 – 6 Monday afternoon because I have a presidents council meeting – but I could from 11 am to 4 and after dinner. Tuesday I am free after 3:15.

I want to see you dreadfully

Love Edith

Thursday, *probably* January 1916
Wellesley College

Tower Court
Thursday-

Bet dearest -

You certainly are the best old cousin a girl ever had – I just came back from Providence where we have been having a time since Saturday, and found your first letter waiting for me.

Your midnight epistle arrived in this afternoon's mail. Thank you for your news. No I didn't know Ruf* was going over [to France] in May. I knew he hoped to go sometime but he didn't bring the subject up in vacation so I thought perhaps he had dropped the idea. I'm sorry he has water on the knee but if he is fluttering about it can't be very serious so I suppose I don't need to go into mourning yet. Well I can't say I don't care about him any more but I can say that I care less and by golly I'm going to kill it if it is the last act of my life. By the time that man gets back from France he is not going to mean one single thing in my life.

It makes me simply sick not to be on hand for B's wedding so we simply won't discuss that - but don't forget to write me full details.

As for Margaret's [Betty's sister] engagement – I am so excited I don't know what to do!!! I wish I knew Cushing [Wright] better, but so long as she is happy I know he must be a dear – Do try and get her married sometime between March 30 and April 15th so I can be there. And isn't it simply slick about the troops coming home! [It was a false alarm.]

I had a perfectly adorable letter from Larry Noyes** today – guess I will have to fall in love with him.

Providence was simply wonderful – we went to bed early Saturday but Sunday and Monday were perfect riots. Hubby is better looking than ever and he certainly does play up well when anybody is feeling high. We got into a most fearful roughhouse and they wiped me all over the floor till I am literally black and blue but anyway it was fun. And I have decided to go to our Prom after all and I am taking Stan Hawkes, Yale '18 who came home on the train with me as far as Chicago – His best friend is engaged to one of my best friends who is chairman of the Prom committee and the four of us will be playing around together. Friday there is dinner at ΦΣ and the Prom. Saturday we are going to the Country club for Tobogganing and lunch – Then back here for tea dances and dinner at ΦΣ after which we are going to town [Boston] to the theater and a supper and dance at the Copley and Sarah and I are going to spend the night at Grandma's [Fanny Baker Ames]. On Saturday an adorable young ΦΣ married Alumnae is having the four of us down for supper and there the boys have to go back to New Haven [Yale] on the Midnight. If you get a salubrious opportunity you might drop a word of all this to friend [Rufus] Rand for I told [him] at Christmas that I didn't think I would go to Prom. That's where I fool him. Also if you get a chance tell him something about the party in Providence and "a man whom I always speak of as Hubby" – It will do him good for I verily believe he thinks I refuse all invitations when he isn't around.

Which reminds me – I told you didn't I about the man at Christmas vespers – well he got a girl I knew to introduce him and now I can't get rid of him. He has asked me to all their law school dances for the rest of the year – and when he doesn't come he telephones.

The latest manifestation was a book on (of all things but I had manifested interest in the subject) aviation. Now don't you think that is funny.

Well dear, I'm pretty blue about Ruf but I suppose I'll get over it. Goodness knows I have enough to do –

Best love

Ede

And please do write me what you know because I am not going to write Ruf anymore and I want to know who he will fall for next.

---

*Leila noted that Rufus Rand joined the Lafayette Escadrille, a unit of the French Aéronautique Militaire. Named in honor of the Marquis de

Lafayette, hero of the American and French revolutions, it was composed principally of American volunteer pilots flying fighters. As the French helped the Americans, so the Americans helped the French. Ruf's daughter, Kate, graduated Bryn Mawr 1945, became a strong feminist, and then a founding editor of *Mademoiselle* magazine.

**Larry Noyes lived in the same neighborhood in St. Paul as Betty and was a close family friend 'always.'

Postmarked **January 12, 1917**
Wellesley College

Wellesley
Thursday

Dearest Bet: –

I am at the tea room awaiting lunch so I haven't time for a letter and anyway I have nothing particular to tell you except that I love you – but I want to tell you about a brother of Frances Fargo's. Carl by name, who is working at Foot Schulge[sp?] and living at the Y.M.C.A. He is about 19 or 20 and is very nice and quite lonely. So I told Fran to tell him to call on you – you don't mind do you?

Best love
Edith

I am getting on splendidly without R – really too busy to think much about him.

Charles 'Willie' 'Charley' Wilberforce Ames
(1855-1921)
m. 1883 **Mary Inches Lesley**
(1854-1929)

Charles 'Les' Lesley Ames
(1884-1969)
m.1917 **Linda Worthington Baker**
(1893-1985)

Margaret Ames
(1885-1956)
m.1917 **Cushing Frederick Wright**
(1879-1971)

Catharine Ames
(1887-1947)
m.24 Sep 1910 **Samuel 'Epes' Turner, III**
(1884-1945)

Alice Ames
(1889-1976)
m.1917 **Bronson Crothers M.D.**
(1854-1959)

Elizabeth 'Betty' Ames
(b. 12 Aug 1894, d. 5 Mar 1990)
m.1922 **Norris Dean Jackson**
(1895-29 Sep 1990)

Theodore Gordon Ames
(1898-1969)
m. 1927 **Barbara 'Bee' Holt**
(1905-1998)

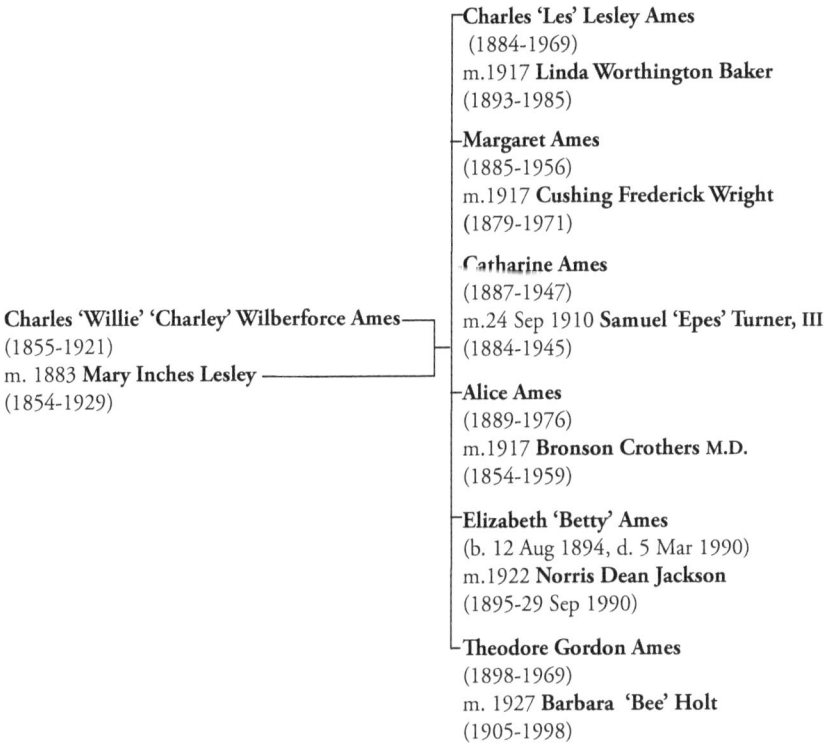

You may need this chart of Betty's immediate family when Edith mentions the weddings of Betty's sisters and brothers.

March 1917
Wellesley College

Lower Court
Wednesday

Dearest Betsy:–

You were a dear to write me when I know you were dead tired and just as busy as you can be. I will repeat that I am exceedingly found of you. I don't know what I have been doing but I have been simply flying. Indeed I haven't arrived at the point of getting a wedding present for Lesley and Linda yet, much less for Margaret and Cushing or Alice & Bronson. Isn't it just too wonderful about them. I don't see how you could keep it to yourself when you know how delighted I would be. I don't know when anything has pleased me more !!!!

Let's see, what have I been doing? Well the same old college stuff of course and lately we have had society initiations and special meetings that have kept me simply flying. Then [Juqunia_sp?] has been at home, sick, and I took her place living with the freshmen in the village for a week. It was wonderful fun and the children were adorable to me but it meant just so much extra to do and extra responsibility. As for frivolity, there have been a couple of dances and a great many movie parties lately and that is about all.

But joy, and rapture, Easter vacation begins a week from day after tomorrow. I am going to Washington [D.C.], stopping over in New York for dinner and the theater with Larry [possibly Noyes or Tighe] and taking the midnight on. By that time the Crocketts will have moved to their summer house which is just outside the city. So my address from Mar 31st to April

*10th will be c/o D.C. Crockett, Silver Springs, Maryland. Do write me there
and tell me all you know. Larry is coming down to Washington on the 5th
and* [will] *stay five days at his aunt's and as he has nothing to do except,
as he says "to climb the monument and drive up and down in an open
Victoria"* [sports car convertible], *we expect to enjoy ourselves together. By
the way you might drop a judicial suggestion of that to R.R.R. if you get a
chance to do it very casually.*

*Skizz and I went to town on a movie bot this afternoon and one of
the films was all about a young aviator named Rand Calder, one cheerful
scene had his aeroplane fall and land in a tree, pitching him out on his head,
which was almost too much for me. Skizz says her arm is out of commission
for life the way I maltreated it. But I am recovering* [from Ruf] *Betty, really
I am. The only thing is that I rather dread living in the same place with him*
[Paris or Minneapolis?] *and seeing him everywhere I go. I'm so afraid I will
get it again!*

*Betty Mayo-Smith called me up last week and we went to Keith's and
had a fine time just like the old days. I think getting away from her mama
is going to be the salvation of that girl. She seems more natural and jolly
already and I'm so glad. Edith McHenry simply raved about Bob Noyes
at the wedding – said he was the only clear-minded person in the house.
Indeed she couldn't say enough about how wonderful he was.*

*All I can think about or dream about now is vacation. And thirteen
weeks from now I expect to be graduated with a B.A. to my credit. Dear, you
certainly will have to take me under your wing next year it is going to be so
queer.*

*And isn't this war situation terrific. I don't know where we are coming
out – I simply can't bear the idea of staying here and going to school if*
[the] *U.S. is going into it actively. Do let me know where Bronson* [Betty's
brother-in-law] *is and whether he has sailed.*

*Best love to all the family – and tell Cushing. I certainly am going to
write to him soon.*

As ever,
Otto

Late Spring, 1917
Wellesley College

Edith is about to graduate from Wellesley. Fellow seniors are becoming engaged to be married. This phenomenon of choosing a spouse before graduating from college was still commonplace when I was a graduating senior at Wheaton College in Massachusetts, still all women in 1973.

Tuesday,

Dearest Betsy: —

It certainly does seem a grand and glorious occasion when I hear from you again. I am so very fond of you.

I went on a swell bot with your young brother last Saturday down at the elegant resort "Revere Beach." We rode on the roller coaster and chewed gum and saw the side show and poor Ted is eternally disgraced because some of his friends saw him down there with a woman in tow.

Ever since then it has rained and rained, indeed it is still at it. Yesterday I spent in town with a young alumna doing some shopping for Phi Sigma but it ended in our lunching at the Touraine and spending the afternoon at the movies. Today more rain! I have a fearfully busy day ahead of me with a meeting from 5 to 7:30 and a caller from 7:30 till the bell puts him out at 9:45.

Tomorrow, praise be is a holiday and the above mentioned young alumna and her young husband are taking Skizz and myself to Braeburn for luncheon and the state championship tennis. And a year ago today Ruf and I went to New York! Well, I am glad I haven't got that year ahead of me again. There are only two more days of classes but I shall not start for home until June 22nd because I really think I had better stay over for commencement and then I might as well stay two extra days for two weddings. Next week I am going over to Betty's to stay from Monday till Saturday – won't that be fun for me. I'm so glad for a chance to re-make her acquaintance

I don't know a bit of gossip to pass on to you – everybody around college is announcing their engagements – three new senior ones this week, but that is getting so commonplace that nobody pays any attention to them any more.

I am so crazy to get home and put my finger into the Twin City pie again, and to see you too!

Best love — Ede

———————————

The US joined allies Britain, France and Russia to fight World War I on April 6, 1917.

May 22, 1917
Wellesley College

History Conference
Thursday
May 22nd
'17

Dearest Betsy –

I feel as if you and I had broken off family relations – but I know you must be simply swamped with work – I wish I could get home and get to work too. The academic side of my work here is practically over but I have to stop on or finish up the other things. Also there are to be two weddings the two days after college classes, which I plan to stay for; so I ought to get home about the 25th and I am planning to bring Sarah Ladd with me because her fiancé is at the Fort [Snelling]* and of course she wants to see him. I don't know how long she is going to stay but I hope to keep her most of the summer.

I spent a night with Betts not long ago. She and Richmond seem to have recovered from being sloppy. They are simply sweet together and Bett has gone back to being the best side of herself. I have some time off during exams and I am going to stay about a week with her and get re-acquainted with her. Richmond of course is away all day and drills two evenings a week so she is a good deal alone.

Larry has gone into the naval Reserve and is very comfortably settled at Newport and seems awfully pleased about it. Everybody has departed, except the few who are staying in the Harvard camp this summer. I went to town yesterday to luncheon, theater, and tea, with one of them but that, I think will be about the last occurrence of the kind this year. Even Wellesley is mobilized. I get up at 6:30 and go to bed at 10:30, and don't eat between meals and have to be fearfully neat, etc. etc. It isn't doing any particular good but it seems to satisfy the administration. Oh dear, it's discouraging, isn't it?

Do write and tell me what is going on at home.

This isn't a particularly cheerful letter, but there is a rabid war discussion going on in this class and it somewhat distracts my attention. Do write me soon.

Best love
Ede.

That was a lov-ally picture of the Hasting's Bridge you sent me.

---

*"Fort Snelling became the induction point for more than 300,000 men and women who joined the armed forces when the U.S. entered World War II in December 1941," said the Minnesota Historical Society website.

"At its height in 1942, the Reception Center was capable of processing approximately 800 recruits each day." [Source: www.historicfortsnelling. org/history/military-history/world-war-ii]

The S.S. Touraine

Paris

⸻⸗⸻

According to Wikipedia, "the *SS La Touraine* was laid down by Compagnie Générale Transatlantique in Saint-Nazaire and launched 21 March 1890. ... At the time she was the fifth-largest steamer in the world" built for France to New York service. "At the outbreak of World War I, the French government took over many of CGT's liners – including *La Touraine* – for a variety of duties."

Photo by John S. Johnston, Library of Congress, Prints & Photographs Division, Detroit Publishing Company Collection, LC-D4-22391, Public Domain. Source: https://commons.wikimedia.org/w/index.php?curid=4215600.

February 15, 1918
Mid-Atlantic aboard the *Touraine*

Edith graduated from Wellesley College in 1917 with a Bachelor of Arts degree. A Minneapolis newspaper article stated that she "made her debut the same year."

The next two letters are from Betty. They were saved by her daughter Kitty. Betty and Edith sailed to France on the *S. S. Touraine* in February of 1918. Betty describes their passage.

A Bord de "Touraine"
February 15th, 1918

Dearest Mother and Father—

Seventh day out and my first letter to you! Well, I know that you won't be surprised for I promised to be dead as a door nail for days after the hurried months at home.

The only <u>English</u> *book I've read has been one of those tiny, dime novelly, short story ones and a little bit of Berta Ruck's book that Alice and Bronson sent to 'dear little Betty!" — I haven't written any letters at all — Life has been just incredibly lazy, we've eaten, walked and slept. The most interesting amusing part of the day has been our French lesson from two to four — can you believe it? Well the reason is that our teacher is about the most charming, fascinating, thoroughly delightful person imaginable — a* *perfectly wonderful French Naval Officer. He's of the Milly-Rae Brown type only much sweeter (not sicky but with more depth - ahem - I just put all that to make you roar - but he is a <u>dream</u> <u>really</u>.) <u>Any how</u> five of us belong to the class; we take turns reading and he corrects our accent; we learn a lot. Then he reads and it is <u>superb</u>! — But I should go back to the beginning.*

It wasn't so bad leaving New York as I expected - we didn't have to dissolve into tears at all. I felt <u>much</u> worse before I left St. Paul and before I got to the dock than I did at the time. Tho' it wasn't a joyful moment. I'm only just beginning to realize that we're going to France after these months of hoping to go. — Our stateroom, like many others, is a fright - terrible stuffy little tenement with no room for turning around. We sit up as late as possible - go below and sink into such heavy airless sleep that we awaken with difficulty in time for eleven o'clock lunch. We couldn't get second sitting so eat at eleven and six, - with bouillon at four and much private food in between. It's been rough as the dickens yesterday and today so rolly that we must cling hard to the nearest person or object if we expect to be anywhere but in the gutter, (professional term forgotten). As it is we've all sprawled several times - which give much pleasure to the onlookers. The second morning out Edith went on the sick list with half the people on board. She's fully recovered now except for occasional moments of peagreen-ness. There's great excitement for many waves come up onto our deck - what must the poor steerage do!

I hate to think of what anxious days you are having at home for I know how dreadful it is to have someone on the sea now-a-days. Up to yesterday I was so tired that I felt quite hopeless and forlorn about our landing safely. — The odds seem so terribly against a steamer. It certainly is a very scary business. Everyone is pretty pessimistic! I guess we'll sleep out from tonight on. — I'm going to write to the other members of the grand famiglia Ames now — so au revoir —

A thousand hugs and kisses, dearest Mother and Father from your devoted Betty.

You are <u>so</u> <u>good</u> about letting me come!

February 18, 1918
Mid-Atlantic aboard the *Touraine*

A Bord
Monday
February 15th, 1918

Dearest All of you —

Isn't it terrible to clump you like this but it must be done — you who
have crossed since the war know what an ocean voyage is like — in spite
of everything I've enjoyed it immensely but how much the people who
in normal times hate it feel! As I've said before our staterooms are fierce
little holes, which have grown so airless by now that we have given up
entertaining many people at tea etc — the past three nights in fact Ede and
I, along with an increasing number each night, have slept in our steamer
chairs, meaning about three or four hours sleep and bushels of amusement
which we'll never forget. It takes so long to get comfortable in your clothes,
with a grimy white pillow and two rugs. Forlorn figures wander past
occasionally, life savers (<u>not</u> our superior confidence giving kind), rugs,
etc., dangling after them. After ten of us sitting out on deck under the most
glorious kind of sky, clear stars and half full moon, we finally bundled up
for bed forward, not under cover, five of us. [At] five o'clock a motley crew
of deck hands wash the deck so waterily that the steamer chairs nearly float

around. At five thirty the three surviving members of the party arose, and with many others saw the <u>loveliest</u> pink sunrise — oh so wonderful. And the much dreaded Bay of Biscay where they said the enemy lurks is smooth as glass. Just before turning in this morning early I went below — such a sight! people sleeping <u>everywhere</u> even on the threshold of the dining salon! – and oh how squalid it was this morning — and the air — Scuse me teacher — words can't describe it — and cutting it was out of the question I pity the poor people who will awaken with difficulty before noon and feel as though they'd been drugged. It's been a great old adventure all this, which I wouldn't have missed for anything. The hour is now seven so forgive me if I burst the doors open into the breakfast room.

Love and kisses from Betty.

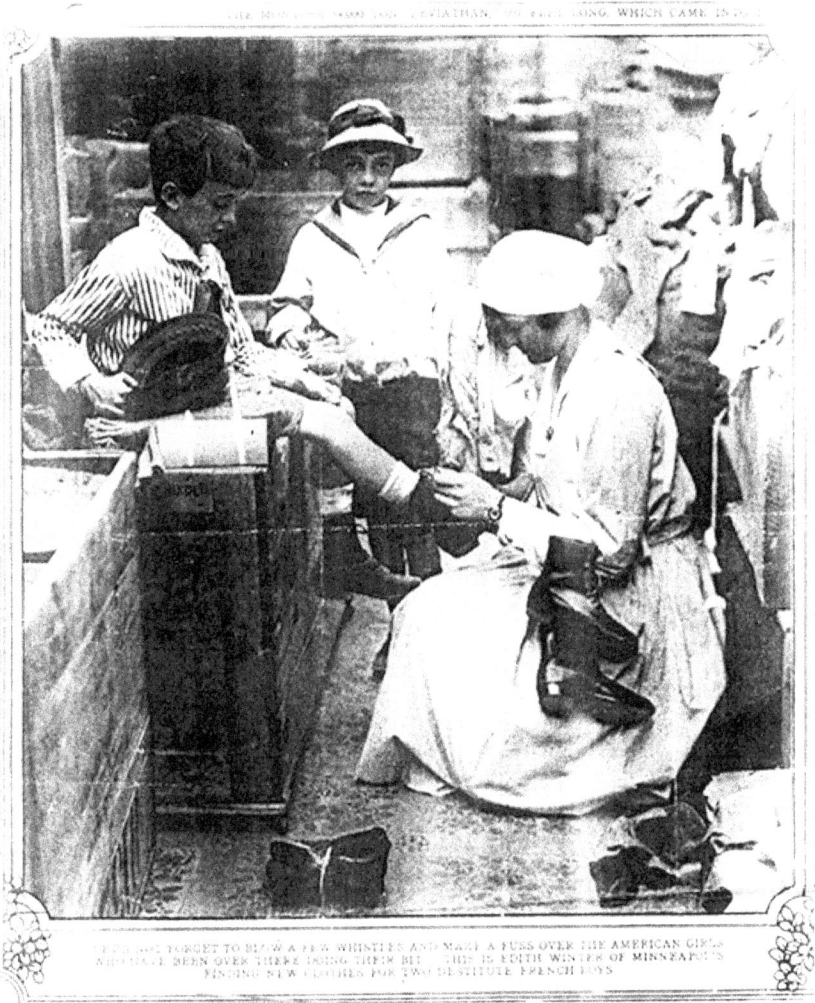

One of the Minneapolis newspapers published the above photo. The caption reads, "Let's not forget to blow a few whistles and make a fuss over the American girls who have been over there doing their bit. This is Edith Winter of Minneapolis finding new clothes for destitute French boys."

The next section features extracts of letters Edith wrote to her mother, Alice, who was in Minneapolis. Alice compiled and typed them up. Carbon copies made their way into the attic at 501 Grand Avenue. These inserts are the only source we have for Betty and Edith's activities during this time period. Since they shared living accommodations, they did not write to each other.

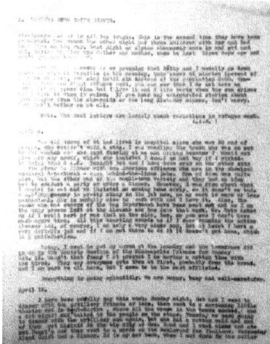

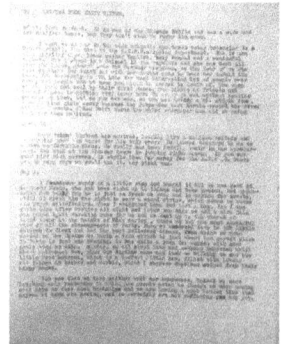

EXCERPTS OF LETTERS FROM EDITH WINTER.

March 26, 1918
Paris, France

You would have laughed if you could have seen me this afternoon, perched on a tool box on the running board of a camion [small truck]. *Flying down the Rue du Rivoli, up the rue de la Paix and down the Grand Boulevard to the Gare du Nord. There was a gang of evacuated refugees and the A.F.F.W.* [American Fund for the French Wounded] *was sending them clothing. So I as official reporter was sent along. The poor things were too pathetic – mostly women and children. We joined two long tables down the center of a long cellar bedroom in the Gare* [du Nord] *and piled up the contents of our bales, then tried to suit everyone at once – dresses, suits, shoes, skirts, and bath-robes for the women (they* [the widows] *mostly wanted black, poor things) stockings and caps for the men, stockings and undies and dresses for the children and safety-pins, handkerchiefs, soap and towels for everyone. We worked till after half-past five and then packed what was left away for the 500 more who are expected in tomorrow morning.*

    All the papers have published it, so I suppose there is no reason for my *not mentioning the German gun*, which has been shelling Paris from 65 miles. Well, it isn't half as serious as I am afraid it sounds in the American papers and it doesn't seem to do much harm. At first, (Saturday) everyone thought it was a daylight raid* [from a high-altitude Zeppelin. There was no sound of an airplane or gun] *and Ruf, who happened to be in town, beat it out and got his machine* [airplane] *and went up to look for the Boche*** [German]. *He went up to 5,800 meters, and then reported that there was nothing up there. Just as he said it – zip – came an explosion quite near by, so naturally his officers laughed him in the face, so he had his machine filled up and went up again until he could hardly breathe, still no Boche. Soon after that they discovered it was shell not bombs. However nobody pays any attention to it any more. Mrs. Lathrop*** gave us all free permission to leave Paris if we wished, but of course no one is going and today's news is better. My boss, Mrs. O'Shaugnessy, came on the job for good today, so from now on I expect only the more mechanical part of the work. Still I love it and it will be good training for me, if I ever want a journalistic job après la guerre* [after the war]. *The man who runs the printing establishment is an Englishman, his foreman, with whom I hold my councils, is a black Indian and all the printers are French but somehow the thing works out and I am learning proof-reading. Tomorrow night Bet and I start canteening for the refugees at the Gare du Nord from 7 P.M. to 2 A.M. every alternate night.*

---

*The Paris Gun, as the German weapon became known, was employed between March and August of 1918. It had a range of 81 miles. When the American's stepped up the offensive, the Germans destroyed the gun to keep the Americans from obtaining it. This gun was different from Big Bertha.

**According to a 1916 article in the *New York Times* magazine, the derogatory term for Germans during WWI, 'boche', was an abbreviation of 'caboche', French slang for 'thick-headed,' or 'slow-pated.'

***Mrs. Benjamin Lathrop was the President of the Board of Administration of the American Fund for French Wounded in France.

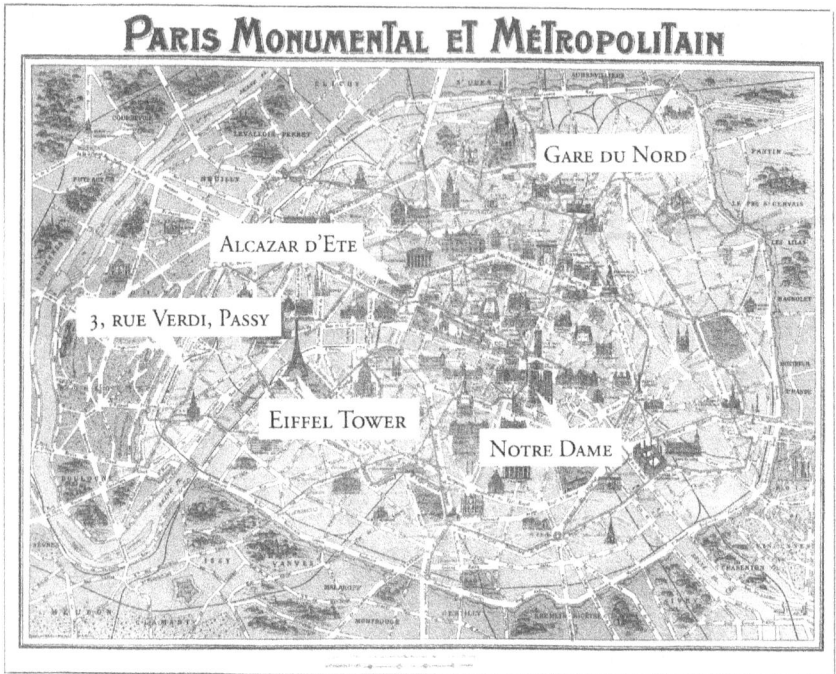

The map above, drawn sometime between 1900 and 1910, shows the location of the Alcazar d'Ete. The girls later move to an apartment at 3, rue Verdi in Paris' Passy district

March 31, 1918
Paris, France

Mr. Arnold Swift of the Premium hams has asked if he might bring some of the Paris newspaper correspondents to call on me, so you see I am getting to be quite the literary lady. But to go back to the cellar of the Gare du Nord. You see thousands of people are being evacuated from the regions where the fighting is going on and they come pouring through Paris. Some stop to sleep in this big cellar room and some we simply feed and pass on to other stations to be sent south. All the organizations are sending down volunteer workers in shifts and Bet and I were there from 12:45 A.M. to 8:45 A.M. today. We give them coffee, or beer or chocolate, all cooked by us, and slices of corned-beef or cheese. The first night I was there, thousands came through and I washed cups in cold water for two solid hours just as fast as I could go and for three hours cut corned-beef as fast as I could. Last night, after a train-load of 1500, things were quieter for a while and *being provided with cards, we sat on boxes and played "Bridge" a while. An orphan asylum came through and we put one little apple-cheeked boy upon the table and he sang "It's a Long Way to Tipperary" with a strong Cockney accent and a French pronunciation. The air in that place is terrific —underground, no air, and thousands of peasants. Three women have had babies there and there are loads of sick children and old men and women, some on stretchers and it is all too tragic. This is the second time they have been evacuated. One woman the other night had three children with her and had lost five on the way. Last night an Alpine chausseur* [member of the elite mountain infantry of the French army] came in and sat and sat, hoping to find his father and mother, whom he lost three days ago and can't get any track of.*

Work at the Alcazar* is so pressing that Betty and I usually go down there as soon as possible in the morning, take about 45 minutes instead of 2 hours at noon, and stay until six instead of the regulation 5:00. Combining that and night refugee work, you can see that I do not have an awful lot of spare time but I love it and I like Paris when the sun shines and I like it when it rains. If you hear any exaggerated stories about much danger from the air-raids or the long distance cannon, don't worry. They don't bother us at all.

---

*The Alcazar d'Ete on Avenue Gabriel near the Champs Elysees served as the Paris Depot for the American Red Cross and American Fund for French Wounded during World War I. The former theater and restaurant was turned into a bustling dispensary and clinic. A report to the Red Cross written in 1917 described the Alcazar's previous existence:

"The theatre is one of the relics of changing Paris life. It is older than the Republic and remembers the famous Mabille, where our grandfathers — but let us hope not our grandmothers — danced and flirted. A Bouillon was added to the theatre for the Exhibition of [18]89. This was rebuilt later and became one of the best-known restaurants of Paris, V Alcazar d'Ete. Here you could dine indoors or out, surrounded with soft-glowing candles, snowy linen, Japanese lanterns, sparkling glass and silver, hats at every angle, feathers of every colour, wraps of every shade, gleaming shoulders and flashing eyes, rouge and powder ad libitum; while a dozen singers and dancers awaited your pleasure on the out-of-door stage."

April 4, 1918

One old woman of 85 had lived in hospital since she was 52 and of course, she couldn't walk a step. I was wheeling the truck she was on out to the camion and she kept fussing at me and crying because I would not give her any snuff, which she insisted I could go and buy if I wished it being then 3 A.M. Tonight Bet and I have been over on the other side of the river to dinner with two American officers who are in the chemical research department – nice behind-the-lines jobs. One of them was quite nice, but the other was of the small-town variety and they had no idea how to conduct a party or order a dinner. However, I was firm about what I wanted to eat and we insisted on coming home early, so it wasn't so bad. Mrs. O'Shaugnessy is pretty steady on the job now, so my work is more or less mechanical. She is awfully nice to work with and I love it. Also, the women who had charge of the bag [comfort sacks] department have been sent out and as I am the only person left at the Alcazar who has done that work, Mr. Gwin asked me if I could sort of run that on the side, too, so you see I don't have much spare time. All this boasting sounds as if I were running the entire Alcazar and, of course, I am only a very minor cog, but at least I have a very definite job and if I am not there to do it, it doesn't get done, which is a satisfaction.

Today, I went to get my apron at the laundry and the laundress did it up in the Society Section of the Minneapolis Tribune *for Sunday Feb. 13. Wasn't that funny? At present I am having a rotten time with the hives. They say everyone gets them at first, probably from the bread, and I am sure we all have, but I seem to be the most afflicted.*

Everything is going splendidly. We are happy, busy and well-cared for.

April 12, 1918

I have been awfully gay this week. Sunday night, Bet and I went to dinner with two Artillery friends of hers, then went to a screaming little theater out in Mont-martre, where all the women in the boxes smoked (one, a fat cigar) and talked to the people on the stage. Tuesday we were going to dinner with the artillery men again, but she had a rotten cold and one of them got mislaid in the big city, so Cec. Read and I went alone and ate out Henri's and then went to a movie on the Boulevard des Italiens. Wednesday Alden Swift had a dinner. He is my new beau, whom I met down in the cellar of the Gare du Nord. He is one of the Chicago Swifts and has a wife and two children there, but they don't seem to worry him much.

I went to dinner in the most adorable apartment today belonging to a Mrs. Churchill, the head of the A.F.F.W. shipping department. She is the slim sporting type, looks rather English, very tanned and a wonderful talker. Her husband is a Colonel in the regulars and she has been all over the place, almost into the Germans trenches, so the four of us who went up there for lunch sat with our mouths open to hear her unfold the tale. You certainly do run into the most interesting lot of people over here, and people who at home you would be scared to death of, you slap on the back and call by their first names. Our circle of friends and acquaintances is getting very large now. We never go out without meeting someone we know, and as you can see, we are not having a bit stupid time. I am feeling quite cocky because the Paris-New York Herald *copied the first article I wrote. Alden Swift knows the chief newspaper man and is going to bring him calling.*

This copy of a copy of a photograph shows the aides in Paris. Edith smiles left of center. Betty is to her left. The man who appears to be hovering above them is sitting on a crate in a lorry [truck].

April 18, 1918

Your friend's husband has arrived, looking like a million dollars and apparently none the worse for his trip over. He leaves tomorrow to go to a nice comfortable place. He really has been awfully lucky in his appointment. The work at the Alcazar keeps me jumping right along. If you see some nice rich persons, do strike them for money for the A.F.F.W. There are so many ways we could use it, any sized sum.

May 2, 1918

I found some candy in a little shop and bought it all up and sent it to Henry Woods, who has been right up in things and been gassed*, but apparently not badly for he is just as fresh as ever and is crying for sweets, still it gives him the right to wear a wound stripe**, which seems to cause him great satisfaction.

Then I staggered home and took a nap, for I was quite done after working all night and later Don Bigelow [of St. Paul]*** and a nice Yale man named Scott Paradise came for us and we went up to the church of Sacré Coeur at the height of the Mont Martre, where we had the most wonderful view of all the chimney-pots of Paris. Then we wandered down to the little Auberge du Cloud and had the most delicious dinner, from which we proceeded to the Casino de Paris – from church to just about the gayest place in Paris in just one evening. It was quite a jump for anyone with such short legs as mine. Sunday, we all slept late and nothing happened until about half-past two, when Don Bigelow came and took me walking to see the little Parc Monceau, which is a perfect little gem, filled with lovely old things in bronze and marble, which I suppose Napoleon swiped from their happy homes.

You see that we lack neither work nor amusement. Indeed we were laughing only yesterday to think how people acted as though we were coming over here to face such hardships and we are having a much better time than anyone at home are having, and we certainly are not suffering any yet.

---

*According to Wikipedia, the Germans used tear gas and mustard gas to "demoralize, injure, and kill entrenched defenders," Because of the gas, some historians refer to World War I as the "chemist's war." The weapon caused less than two percent of combat deaths. Use of it diminished after the allies developed effective gas masks.

Miss Anna Murray Vail, who served on the Board of Administration for the Paris Depot along with Betty, visited the A.F.F.W. dispensary in

La Meuse, which is near France's border with Luxembourg. She wrote, "All that morning the wounded came pouring in, many burnt by a new asphyxiating gas, a gas that is imperceptible at first; but that burns after having impregnated clothing and lungs. Its action is so corrosive that some of the nurses told me their arms had been badly blistered while dressing the wounds

**Soldiers wore wound stripes on the sleeves of their outer garments placed above the left cuff and below the 'good conduct stripes.' The man in the middle of the photo below earned one stripe for being wounded once and the man to his left earned three. Image source: http://www.worldwar1postcards.com/real-photographic-ww1-postcards.php.

***Leila said that Don Bigelow was another neighbor of 501 Grand Avenue. Later he became a U.S. career diplomat.

Edith's mother typed the next set of 'extracts' using a slightly different format. I am confused about timing. Edith refers to the beginning of the American offensive. However, according to my research, the first 'major offensive' by the Americans did not start until September 12, 1918. Edith works in an office that is a 'train ride' outside Paris.

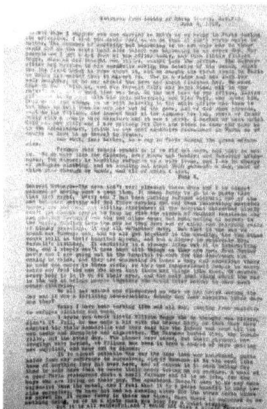

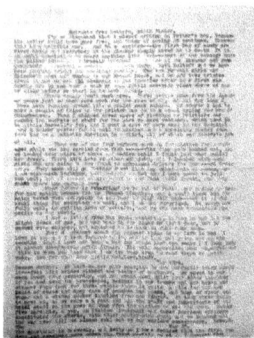

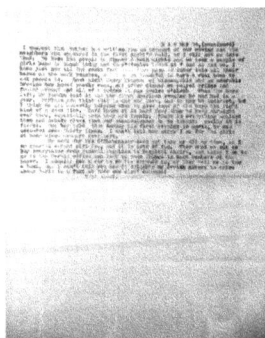

June 5, 1918

Dearest Ma:– I suppose you are worried to death at my being in Paris during the offensive. I wish you could feel as we do that it isn't worth while to bother. The chances of anything bad happening to us are only one in thousands and on the other hand nice things are happening to us every day. For example — I got a lot done at the office today, and then little Ellison Boggs, whom we all thought was killed, walked into the office. The authorities had written to his escadrille [French aircraft squadron] *asking the details of his death, which was the first thing he knew about it, and he caught the first train to Paris to cable his mother that it was not so. She is a widow and has lost her only daughter, so he was afraid the news had about finished her. He came home to lunch with us, and Mrs. Fernald Swift and Major Rice, all in the major's car, and a good time was had. On the way back to the office, Ellison persuaded me to play with him this afternoon, and Miss Vail, who loves him, told me to run along, so we went taxiing to the cable office and then to the bank to tell them he was not out of the game, and we did some errands, went to the Crillon, and landed back at the Alcazar for tea, where we found Betty with a couple more aviators and it was a party. I worked my best until 6:30 and now Betty and I are waiting for Dick and Alden to come and take us to the Ambassadeurs, (which is the most expensive restaurant in Paris so of course we love to go there) to dinner.*

And that, dear Mother, is a day in Paris during the great offensive.

Perhaps this record sounds as if we did not work, and that is not so. We do work like the dickens, over hours and Sundays and Saturday afternoons. The Alcazar is handling refugees as a side issue, and I am in charge of refugees clothing and am sending out about 5000 garments a day, most of which pass through my hands, and all of which I list.

June 9, 1918

Dearest Mother:— The news isn't very pleasant these days and I am almost ashamed of having such a good time. It seems funny to go to a party like that last night. Betty and I had been packing refugee clothes; one of the men had been getting off Red Cross envoys; one had been inspecting hospital wards; one had been out lifting stretchers at the hospital where they simply can't get enough people to keep up with the stream of wounded Americans who are passing through; and the two other women had been acting as nurses in the wards, holding down the men as they came out of ether and carrying pails of bloody dressings. It was all volunteer duty. But that is the way we spend our Sundays now, and we all got together in the evening, the two other women still in their hospital aprons, and had a dinner to celebrate Mrs. Fernald's birthday. It certainly is a strange life, but it is interesting too, and I simply can't come home with things as they are now. Next Sunday Betty and I are going out to the hospital to work, for the Americans are coming in thick, and they are operating 24 hours a day, and sometimes there is only one nurse in three wards, so they use inexperienced people to carry water and feed the men who have lost limbs and things like that. Of course every body is in it up to their eyes, and the only good thing about the war is the way it brings people together who would never bother to know each other otherwise.

We all sat around and discoursed on what we had heard during the day and it was a thrilling conversation. Nobody can lack subjects these days, can they?

Today I have been working like mad all day, jumping from bulletin to refugee clothing and back.

I wrote you about little Ellison Boggs who we thought was killed, didn't I? Well, he has made a hit with the bosses here, so that they have adopted his whole escadrille and they call him the Infant, and send all the men socks and chocolate and cigarettes. The Germans bombed them, the Escadrille, out the other day. The planes were saved, but their personal belongings were burned, so Ellison has been in town a couple of days getting new supplies, and came out to dinner.

It is almost pathetic the way the boys love our apartment, quite aside from any reference to ourselves, simply because it is the most like home of anything they hit over here, and of course it is much better for them to come here than to waste their money taking us on parties. A meal at a good Paris restaurant costs a small fortune and it is no joke for the boys who are living on their pay. The apartment doesn't seem to be any more expensive than the hotel, and I feel that it is a great benefit to many beside ourselves. We have not had an evening alone for the three weeks since we moved in. It seems funny in these war times, when there is supposed to be nothing doing, to be in a state when you long for a quiet evening.

But it is all wonderful, and I would not miss a single experience,

After Mother's Day, 1918

I'm so disgusted that I missed writing on Mother's Day, because the letter could have gone free, and think of saving 25 centimes. However this is a terrible war. And I'm so excited — the first box of candy arrived today and everybody at the Alcazar simply loved me to death. It is an awful temptation to hoard anything like that – sort of the sausage under the pillow idea – but I bravely produced it at tea at the Alcazar and gave everybody a treat. This evening Elizabeth Marks, Ruth Baltuff and we have been playing bridge and munching lustily. The two Farwell girls and Elizabeth went off Sunday to our Epinal Depot, and we are tres tristes [very sad] *about it but we are all planning to get together after our first six months are up and have a week at some little sea-side place where we can be silly before we start in to work again.*

There really isn't much news. Three people gone from the Alcazar means just so much more work for the rest of us, and all day long I have been running around like a poulet sans salade [chicken with her head cut off]. *Of course I had to make a couple of trips to the printer and do the usual typing for Mrs. O'Shaughnessy. Then I shipped seven cases of clothing to Poietiers and packed two baskets of stuff for the Gare du Nord Vestiare, which used to be little Farwell's job, and I sent a case of corn meal to one hospital and a bright poster for the wall to another and a specially packed comfort bag to a pathetic American in a third, all of which was nobody's job at all.*

Then one of our four workers came in for clothes for a refugee child she had carried down from [–?–] *when they were bombed out, and we looked over piles of shoes and undies until I found just what suited her fancy. There were lots of other odd jobs, and I lunched with some girls who are going to the front as ambulance drivers* for the French army. They will go further front than any other unit of women, and I am wild with jealousy, particularly as Bet and I were asked to join the unit, but of course we are* *bound to the Fund till August, and they can't spare any workers now.*

Poor father is "chuffing" [Edith is probably imitating her father's British accent to mean "chaffing"] *to be out of Paris, and having to wait for his special permit for the French trenches, and I can't blame him for being bored when everybody is too busy to play with him – but it is the usual thing for everybody to wait, and I am not surprised. He seems awfully well, is getting lots of exercise, and has the most tremendous appetite in the world.*

I had a letter from Ken Woods yesterday, saying he had had two slight doses of gas, and was back in the lines on light duty, but he seemed very chipper, and expected to be back on full duty soon.

Just at present about the biggest thing in my life is bed. I love it so, and I look forward to it, and if I am not going out in the evening (and I have not been a bit gay these last two weeks) I leap into it almost immediately after dinner. You will appreciate what an awful war this is when you hear that I am too busy even to read Vogue *or* Vanity Fair. *Now for that dear little bed.*

Love, Eduff

---

*The 1917 report from the Red Cross I have been quoting included an article about the women who worked as ambulance drivers for the French Army. They were known as the 'Motor Service.'

"These American girls who do men's work and do it well have appealed to the French imagination and sentimentality. Their task is not an easy one. Long stretches of muddy roads, days of wind and rain, or dust and heat, cleaning, repairing, bruises and heavy responsibilities are their lot.

"Each of our depots has its ambulance and a driver who is sometimes dame de magasin, chauffeuse, ambulanciere and visiteuse rolled into one. Thirty-six hours work on a stretch is not unlikely, for when some big military movement is on and one is called upon to aid in transporting the wounded there can be no refusal and the distributing service of the depot must go on just the same.

"In spite of the hard work there is not one of our depot drivers who would exchange her job for a softer one because nowhere else would she come into such direct contact with the soldier and military life. Immediate results are so encouraging and nothing is like the moral stimulus of the 'front.'"

"To drive for a depot is a reward of merit. Only drivers who have been with the Society for a long time and have been tried out can aspire to the position. Good health and above all steady nerves and staying qualities, are absolutely necessary requirements."

May 23, 1918

Dearest Mother. At last we are chez nous, and we are perfectly crazy about it – feel like brides without the bother of husbands. We moved [to the ground floor of 3, rue Verdi] *in our noon lunch hour yesterday, and you would have split your sides laughing if you had seen the procession, because* [along with] *our trunks and hat boxes and steamer rugs (and for three people there is quite a pile) we had arm loads of coats and many cans of peaches and pears, and bags of flour and sugar and sterno cooker dangling from one finger. It took three taxis to move us, so we were a parade and all the staff and inhabitants of the hotel stood on the pave or hung from the windows to see the show. Madame, five servants, a yap, an Italian lieutenant and three American officers constituted the chorus, with their mouths wide open, and we laughed all the way over till we almost fell out of our various conveyances.*

Love. E.

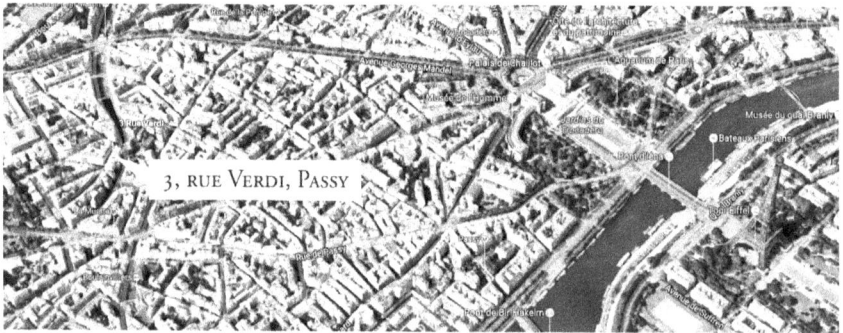

3, RUE VERDI, PASSY

The 3DGoogleMap above shows the location of the girls' apartment at 3, rue Verdi about twelve blocks from the Eiffel Tower [on the right]

Wikipedia describes Passy as "a district or neighborhood in Paris located in the XVIe [Sixteenth] Arrondissement on the Right Bank of the River Seine. It is traditionally home to many of the city's wealthiest residents. ... Passy is known to Americans as the home of Patriot Benjamin Franklin during the nine years that he lived in France during the American Revolutionary War." Honoré de Balzac lived and wrote there, too."

May 26, 1918

The Apartment is heavenly, and Betty and I have decided that the first two days and evenings were worth the first month's rent. I suspect that father has written you an account of moving and the neighbors who appeared in the first night's raid, so I'll not go into that. We have had people to dinner both nights and we took a couple of girls home to lunch today and they 'simplee loved it' and so did we. I know just how all the cooks feel when they have to entertain all their beaux on the park benches, and I am so thankful to have a real home to ask people to. Last night Henry Kingman of Minneapolis and an adorable Brooklyn boy named Jacobs came, and after dinner we played bridge and fooled around and all of a sudden it was twelve o'clock. When the boys left, Mr. Jacobs said it was the first American evening he had had in a year. Perhaps you think this is not war work, and it may be indirect, but I think we are honestly helping when we give some of the boys the right kind of a good time. Lord knows it is hard for them to keep straight over here, especially when they are lonely. There is everything against them and nobody gives them any encouragement to be decent. Really it is fierce. One boy told me that during his first evening in Paris, he was accosted over thirty times. I can't tell how sorry I am for the girls at home whose men are over here.

My work for Mrs. O'Shaugnassy does not take me all the time, so I am general errand girl too, and it is lots of fun. They send me out to buy everything from general supplies to hospital chairs, and today I am to go to the Herald office and look up some things in back numbers of the paper. I usually get a car to do the errands in, or they tell me to take a taxi, and I can't tell you how it delights my Jewish nature to drive about Paris in a Taxi at someone else's expense:

Must scoot.

_____

This is the end of the clips from Edith's letters as recorded by her mother.

August & September, 1918

Betty saved these receipts for food or services purchased while she and Edith were working at the Alcazar. Dated August and September of 1918, their significance eludes me. I cannot figure out what the first one is for. Something was purchased for six francs. A penciled note states "mons screened." The vendor's name 'Chantier' means 'Construction Site.'

The middle item is an 'Individual Food Card.'

The receipt on the right is for the cleaning and repair of the heater in the bath.

Probably **1918**

While the girls were still at the Alcazar, they received this postcard from Lieutenant Alan F. Winslow, a prisoner of war in Germany. According to Leila, he was the brother of an old friend of Betty's from either Boston or St. Paul. I could not decipher the date stamp.

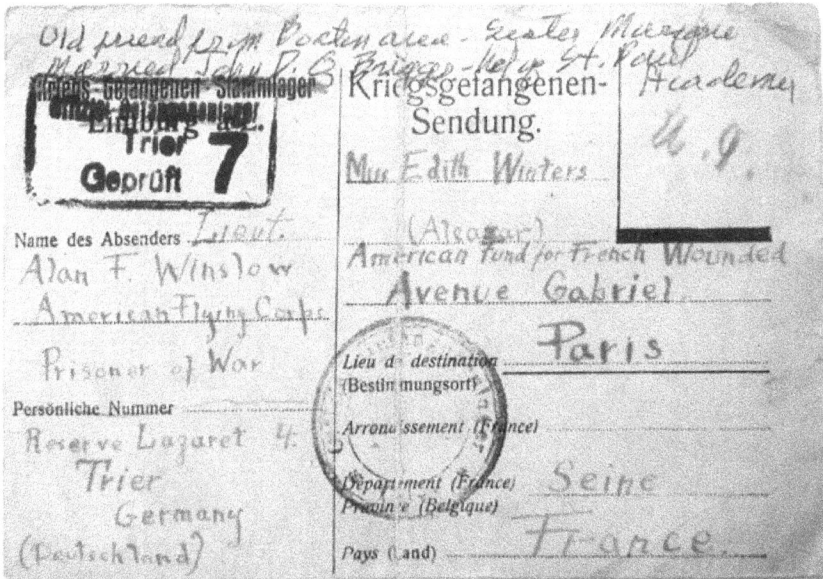

Postmarked: Trier Geprüft 7, Deutschland
Name des Absenders [Name of the sender]: Lieut. Alan F. Winslow
American Flying Corp
Prisoner of War
Kriegsgefangenen-Sendung [POW shipment]: Miss Edith Winters
(Alcazar) American Fund for French Wounded
Avenue Gabriel. Paris
Lieu de destination (Bestin mungsort): Paris
Arrondissement (Frances), Department (France): Siene
Pays (Land/Country): France

Dear Edith and Betty, – Please do not think me imprudent or bold in writing this note and request; I know you won't when you realize I am allowed to write only to civilions[sic], and you are of the few civilions whose address I know in France. As you may know, I am a prisoner, and am in a German hospital with my left arm off – due to an unfortunate aerial battle. I am writing to ask you a great favor, – I have no one else to turn to , – in my transportation to this hospital, certain parts of my clothing were either lost or rendered useless by my wound. Therefore I ask you – (It is a lot to ask of a girl, but I know you will understand the necessities of a case like mine) – to send me a parcel as soon as possible containing the following articles: 2 khaki shirts with collar attached (size 15), 1 brown tie to match, 1 'overseas' cap with aviation colors on piping (size 7¼), 2 pair heavy socks (size 11½). And (if not too embarrassing!) a pair of heavy underwear. I know this is a lot to ask, but you do not know how much your services will be appreciated if you can do this. Also, if you can find them, throw in some cigarettes. And please include in the parcel an account of your expenses, that I may straighten the matter as soon as I am back from confinement. Outside of my arm I am in excellent health and spirits! My arm is healing normally and doing finely. Several months after I am well I expect to be sent back to America as all officers unfit for war are sent back I can not thank you too much for the services I ask of you.

Along the left edge, he wrote
I am sure you understand my predicament. Best thoughts and wishes, always,

Along the right edge, he wrote
P.S. you can best find these articles at 'Old England"

⸻⚬⚬⚬⸻

Edith writes the next letter on a 'lettersheet.' Lettersheets folded to become their own envelopes to save on postal weight. Later, during World War II, when letters were transported by airplanes, lettersheets became known as 'aerograms.'

The young women are now living and working in different places. Betty is still at 3, rue Verdi. Edith, as you will see from her return address, is with Autochir #7, Par [care of] the B.C.M [British Military Corps] outside Paris somewhere.

According to a web article about Clara Davis,* who was also with Autochir #7, these convoys of trucks and ambulances took a position directly behind military divisions. "They moved forward with the division during an attack, and retreated when the division retreated, always on the ready to dash into the middle of the troops to serve and triage** the wounded. One autochir carried enough provisions to sufficiently hospitalize eighty soldiers. In a triage capacity the autochir could accommodate two hundred and fifty wounded. ... There were usually five vehicles: a truck for radiology; another for sterilization; a third for the huts and the removable operating room. The fourth and fifth trucks carried hospital equipment."

Autochir #1 was organized by Robert Proust, the brother of novelist Marcel Proust (1871-1922). Both men were the sons of Professor of Medicine and Medical Officer Adrien Proust. In August of 1915 – three years before Edith wrote this letter – a limit was placed on the number of autochirs to twenty-one.

There were 'light' versions of autochirs. Since Edith's address at Saint Roch is not on the front line, I am guessing she is either working for a light version or that Saint Roch was where Autochir #7 received its mail, or both.

――――――――――――

*Source: https://claradavis.wordpress.com. Clara Davis later became a pediatrician in Chicago. In 1928, she published her revolutionary report that children self-select what is good for them to eat if provided with nutritious choices.

**Triage means to assign the degrees of urgency to a wounded patient.

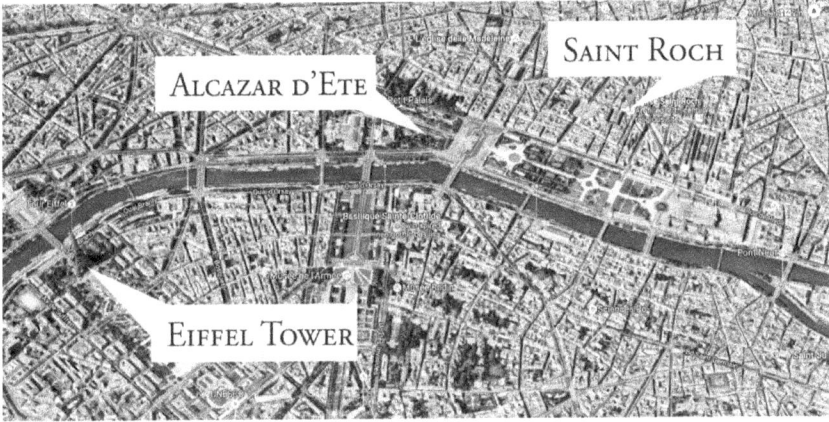

Postmarked: 21 IX 1918 [September 21, 1918]
20:30 [8:30 p.m.]
Paris, Saint Roch

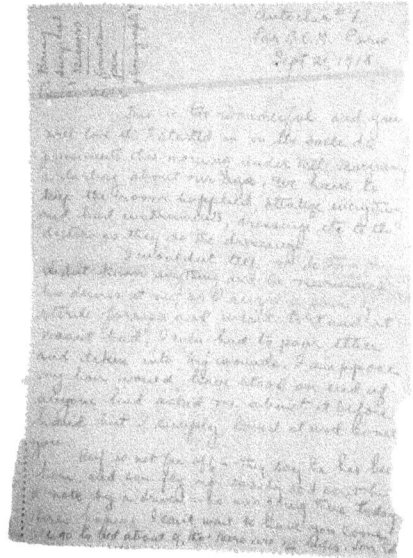

Envelope side, From:
E.A. Winter
Autocher #7
Par B.C.M Paris

> To: *Miss Elizabeth Ames*
> *Alcazar d'Eté*
> *Avenue Gabriel*
> *Paris*

Letter side: Edith wrote in the top margin:
Bring surgical scissors | fountain pen | phonographs

> *Autocher #7*
> *Par B.C.M. Paris*
> *Sept 21, 1918*

Betsy dear: –
*   This is too wonderful and you will love it. I started in the salle des pausimento this morning under Mlle Margianey, a darling about our age. We have to keep the room supplied, sterilize everything, and hand*

instruments, dressings etc to the doctors as they do the dressings.

I wouldn't tell the doctors I didn't know anything and he murmured his desires at me, so I seized a pair of sterile forceps and went to it and it wasn't bad! I even had to pour ether and dakin [Dakin's Solution, a strong antiseptic] *into big wounds. I suppose my hair would have stood on end if anyone had asked me about it beforehand but I simply loved it and so will you.*

Ruf is not far off – they say he has been here, and can fly up easily so I sent him a note by a driver who was going there today. Here's hoping. I can't wait to have you come. We go to bed about 9, tho' There are no rules.

Love Ede.

September 22, 1918
Paris

Envelope side:
E.A. Winter
Autocher #7
BCM

To: *Miss Elizabeth Ames*
Alcazar d'Été
Avenue Gabriel
Paris

Letter side:

Autocher #7
Par B.C.M. Paris
Sept 22, 1918

Betsy dearest: –
    Just a line to say everything is going well and I still love it.
    This morning I worked again in the "Salle des pausements," and this afternoon I went joy riding on a Fiat Camion and had tea with some English women down the line and came home in the rain with an arm load of flowers.

Tomorrow, because Miss Scott isn't back yet – I am to have the 'salle' all alone, and we are to have an operation. Help. But you will adore it and it is just the kind of a job for you. I have talked so much about you they are all looking forward to your coming.

Love Ede

October 15, 1918
Paris

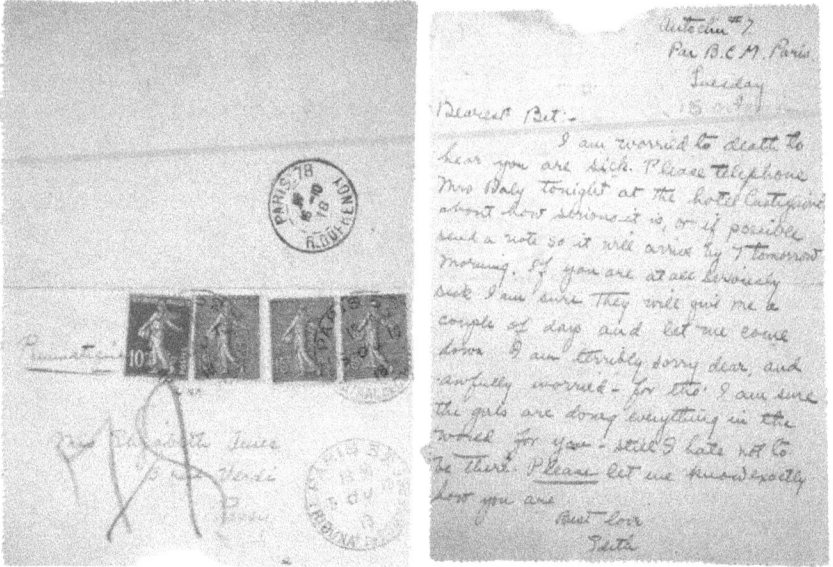

As you can see from the image above, there are two postmarks on this lettersheet. Edith is still with Autochir #7 and Betty is still at 3, rue Verde in Passy.

A stamp on the back of the envelope reads:
Paris 78 R. Dufrenoy
16-10 18 [16 October 1918]

A second stamp by the address reads:
Paris 32 Tribunal Decommerce 18 30 1
5 du 10 18 [15 October 1918]

Edith wrote:

Prenmatique
Miss Elizabeth Ames
3 rue Verdi
Passy

Letter side:

Autocher #7
Par B.C.M. Paris
Tuesday

Dearest Bet: –
   I am worried to death to hear you are sick. Please telephone Mrs.
Daly tonight at the Hotel Castiglione [a fashionable hotel in Passy] *about*
how serious it is, or if possible send a note so it will arrive by 7 tomorrow
morning. If you are at all seriously sick I am sure they will give me a couple
of days and let me come down. I am terribly sorry dear, and awfully
worried for tho' I am sure the girls are doing everything in the world for you
– still I hate not to be there. Please let me know exactly how you are.
                              Best love
                              Edith

October 17, 1918
France

Postmark on the envelope side:

Paris XVI – Place ____?___ [possibly de Opin]
20:45 [8:45 pm]
17 • X | °18 [17 October 1918]

Edith wrote:

Miss Elizabeth Ames
3 rue Verdi
Paris XVI

Letter side:

October 16th 1918

Betsy dear: –

Our orders have come to go to St Quentin - Thank the Lord. Still I'm sorry not to be going to Champagne. All mail for me had better be addressed par B.C.M. from now on as it won't be so easy to get to Paris. I do so hate to think of you sick down there!!!

There isn't any news otherwise. I have a ward in the fracture service and while my men are very nice I don't like it as well as the 'salle des pausements' and I miss you like the devil. Do make everybody write to me

– and don't get married or do anything peculiar without giving me warning.
When you come up bring a pencil which is red at one end & blue at the
other, or a red one & a blue one, & a watch with a second hand.
Love. Ede.

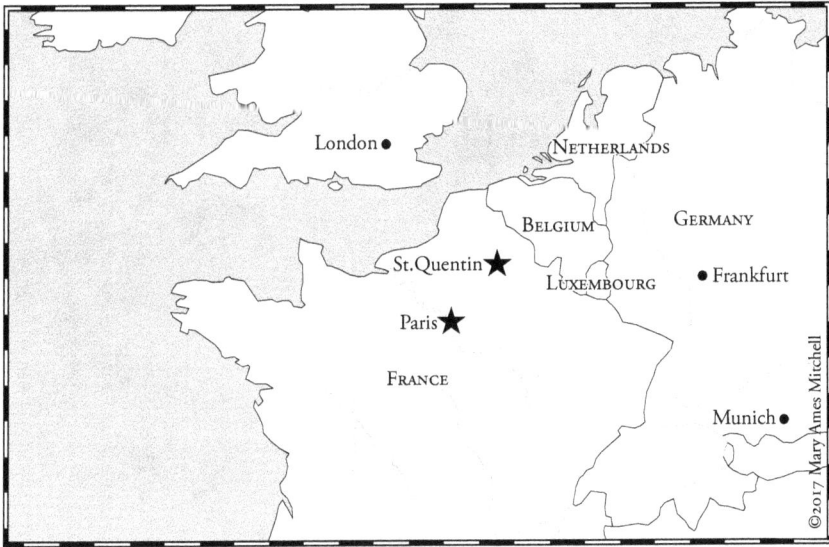

Location of St. Quentin northeast of Paris.

1918
France

Written in the top margin:
Either keep mail, or take it to Hotel Castiglioni and leave it c/o Mrs. Daly's
Unit [where Betty worked].

Autochir #7. Aux Armées
S.P.164
1918

Betsy dearest.

After that one bunch of mail from Ed Baker and Franc, and Ralph
Jacobs, you, Douglas Cameron (who by the way is in a hospital in England
with a bullet through his leg - not serious) I haven't had any. In fact none
has come to the Autochir for 2 days and you had better [not] *send it*
[through the] *B.C.M, but by the S.P. as above until we move — as it looks as*
if we were going to do soon for they evacuated all of my men this afternoon
and we had a hectic morning doing all their dressings. Now that they are
gone we have demenagéd [relocated] *my salle des pausements and I expect*
tomorrow they will put me into the wards.

Things continue to go splendidly – Fowler and Nora Saltonstall are
away, and so are lots of others for there is so little work they are taking
permissions, but Muna Manziarly is my boss and my standby and all the
others are awfull[sic] nice. Muna's father is French and her mother Russian

and she is so full of life. She runs all day long and talks at the top of her voice. Her name begins with Desirée Stephanie and then takes in about ten more on the way to its finish. She is only 21 and you will like her lots. I never wear a corset anymore and my chief idea of dressing up is to change my coiffe before dinner. So you can see I am losing the Paris touch.

My dear Ted Baker was too darling. He said he couldn't 'get over it,' but if I said I was just trying to be nice to him because I was sorry for him to say so and he would try not to make an utter fool of himself. — He was assigned to the 96th Squadron and the letter was written Sept 12th so I am awfully worried on account of that rumor. Do make the boys find out about it! I wrote and asked Ted Brown to do what he could to find out whether he was all right.

My dear the food is wonderful. Fried chicken and stuffed tomatoes, and last night petit suisse & jam. Clemeuce Crafts appeared like a ghost in the darkness last night, having driven 50 kilometers to see me and another girl who is sick here. She is terribly thin and apparently they are having a rotten time for everyone fights. Miss Hathaway just got the Croix de Guerre. I got your letter written on the train from Reimes – Love to all, Ede.

November 11, 1918

The First World War ended on November 11, 1918, with the signing of the Peace Treaty of Paris. Nine million combatants and seven million civilians had died during the struggle.

November 16, 1918

Five days later, the *Minneapolis Evening Sun* published this article about the American Fund for French Wounded.

Copyright, Underwood & Underwood.

Miss Enid Dessau of New York and Miss Edith Winter of Minneapolis, secretaries of the American Fund for French Wounded at the Paris Headquarters of the A. F. F. W., which is affiliated with the American Red Cross.

Doing Their Bit Over There

[Caption] Miss Enid Dessau of New York and Miss Edith Winter of Minneapolis [on the left], secretaries of the American Fund for French Wounded at the Paris Headquarters of the A.F.F.W., which is affiliated with the Red Cross.

Let's Not Forge the French

They are working hard these days at the shipping department of the American Fund for French Wounded. There is such a tragic difference in Christmas for the French soldiery and that for our own beloved American troops overseas. Here wives and mothers and sweethearts and cousins and maiden aunts and friends are positively in anguish because shipping space is so precious that only one little package a soldier may go overseas; but in France, that has lost so much during more than four years of invasion, there are thousands of soldiers who have no home folk left after the cruel German occupation to prepare a Christmas gift for the tired soldiers in the faded blue uniforms or to worry because they cannot send more and still more.

But America will not forget them on this fifth Christmas of their tragedy. A visit to the aforementioned shipping department of the A.F.F.W. proves that. At one end stand hundreds of cases full of hospital supplies, civilian garments and surgical dressings ready to be shipped to France. Half empty cases still being packed are at the other end. All about, piled high, are the boxes and bundles that had come in from all parts of the country ...

"But it isn't the great big contributions that come in from our organized committees that most impresses one," said one of the women workers of the fund as she showed a visitor through the big, busy room where other workers were busily bent over great boxes. ... The other day a woman came in bearing a neatly wrapped brown paper parcel. She came up to my desk and said, 'I'm bringing you a gray knitted petticoat for a refugee. It's quite new. I got it last year but I never wore it. I got through last winter without it and I guess I can get through another.' That was all. She turned and left me with the package in my hands. ...

"It is the little things like this, happening every day, that keep our energies at top speed. Physical weariness vanishes and we get new strength. What do we want? What do we need? Oh, we need everything! As Mrs. [Isabel Stevens] Lathrop, our Paris representative [and president], wrote the other day: 'Please send us pajamas, cotton flannel dressing gowns, shirts and socks. Every wounded man must have these before he can get out of bed and the hospitals are full of wounded men.'

"We especially need property bags (small cretonne [canvas] bags which are hung at the head of each bed and in which the men keep their most precious possessions), comfort bags, sometimes called Christmas bags but which are received at all times with almost childish glee by the men who have seen so little of ease and beauty these years.

"The shipping department of the A.F.F.W. is at 541 [corrected in pen to 531] Seventh avenue. If you found you just could not possibly get all the things you planned for your soldier overseas into that ridiculously small Red Cross carton, why not tuck the remnants into a gay cretonne bag and send it through the A.F.F.W. to gladden the Christmas of some lonely poilu [infantry soldier in the French army] in far away France.

December 12, 1918
[Aboard the] *RMS Baltic*, **White Star Line**
[sailing from] **Liverpool, England**

Postcard* of His Royal Majesty's Ship Baltic, *c.1900*

Edith is on her way home and traveling with her father. They are sailing on the *SS Baltic*. Betty is staying in France to help the Fatherless French Children organization which provided for the care of hundreds of orphans.

According to Wikipedia, the *SS Baltic*, built in 1903 for the White Star Line, was the largest passenger ship in the world. The White Star Line "was a highly prominent British shipping company, today most famous for its ill-fated vessel, the *RMS Titanic* and the World War I loss of Titanic's sister ship *Britannic*. ... As a lasting reminder of the White Star Line, modern Cunard ships use the term 'White Star Service' to describe the impeccable level of customer care expected of the company."

Source: Wikipedia via GreatShips.net

The Baltic
December 12, 1918

Dearest Spud:—

Look where we are [arrow pointing to "The Baltic"]. *We saw Keith Merrill in London and were to lunch with them but found we had to catch a 2:10 train. But he sent you all kinds of nice messages and hopes you will go home by England. Then we happened into the railroad carriage with Milly Fowler and found she still had the berth she offered me in her stateroom free – so we decided to try and come on this boat. A military attaché from the Embassy was also in the carriage and he gave father a card to the White Star asking special service and telephone in consul in Liverpool, and so this morning we got down to the steamship office and got busy. The boat was supposed to sail at 9 this morning but didn't leave till noon and we were on her bag and baggage and the consul sent down a man to see we were all right. I am in a nice big outside stateroom with Milly, who has been perfectly wonderful to me, and we have a table of six – father, Milly, the military attaché, Captain Wise of the R.C. (rather Major Boyer's type) and a Canadian Royal Air Force boy who is just out of five months in the hospital and is still unable to use his right arm so I have to cut up his food and fix his potatoe. The boat is simply flooded with princes – mostly aviators both English and American and the prospects are all for big days ahead. For instance, right in front of me is a long dark jem[sic] in one of those heavenly blue new R.A.F. uniforms. Oh Bet, I do so wish you were along. This ought to be a wonderful crossing and I hate like poison to have you miss it. I have missed you every step of the way and you will simply have to come home.*

I forgot to say the military attaché named Captain Wells was an officer of Harvard* for years – Knows everyone in the country, including Les and Ted and has visited Major Olds and the Severances in St. Paul.

Best love,
Ede.

———————————

*Betty's brother Les (Lesley) graduated from Harvard in 1905. Ted (Theodore) will graduate in 1920.

December 19, 1918
The RMS Baltic

December 19th

They say we will be in late tomorrow night or Saturday morning so the party is almost over. It hasn't been a very exciting voyage for there were practically no girls and the ship is absolutely dry; but I have had an awfully good time. I almost fell for a Canadian naval officer who is in love with a girl in England. However we have turned out merely the best friends and Milly Fowler and I have have spent brief intervals of the day playing nurse in his cabin — for he has a touch of flu. I have only had a couple of days

seasickness so I am doing awful damage to the food.

It Robertson — a most attractive Royal Air Force man from St Louis has taken my pen to write you a letter and there are two others helping him so I tremble to think of the result. However, as I told them — you were my friend first.

On board we have.

1. Lady Constance Stuart-Richardson
2. Simon Flexner
3. Percy Haughton
4. August Belmont.
5. Mary Young Craig — of the Castle Sq.

Lady Constance always wears a turban and Russian boots in the morning, sandals and white stockings all night. There is also an amusing Italian

aviator — Conte Carulio de Something who draws the Parisienne pictures and takes the kidding everyone gives him with the most wonderful grace.

We are all sitting around waiting for Ten and Scottie is going to recover from the flu and come up. He has taught me the most gorgeous British naval slang — really Bet — he is a gem — hasn't got a cent, and is the homeliest man God ever made, with the most divine sense of humor. You would love him, and so would I, only I won't.

I feel utterly removed from my life over there. I simply can't concentrate my mind on Ted — Tho' you needn't tell him that — I simply forget him for days at a time — and only

occasionally past and future reoccur to me as things far away and not important enough to be considered. I can't concentrate on Larry either — in fact I am afraid my mind is fading utterly and you will come home to find me tucked away in some asylum.

In fact about the only thought I have is that I love you and wish you were here — as usual.

The Bumps.

December 19th [1918]

*They say we will be in late tomorrow night or Saturday morning so the
party is almost over. It hasn't been a very exciting voyage for there were
practically no girls and the ship is absolutely dry* [no alcohol], *but I have
had an awfully good time. I almost fell for a Canadian naval officer who is
in love with a girl in England. However we have turned out merely the best
friends and Milly Fowler and I have spent brief intervals of the day playing
nursie in his cabin – for he has a touch of flu. I have only had a couple of
days sea-sickness, so I am doing awful damage to the food.*

*Lt Robertson – a most attractive Royal Air Force man from St Louis –
has taken my pen to write you a letter and there are two others helping him
so I tremble to think of the result. However, as I told them – you were my
friend first.*

On board we have.

1. *Lady Constance Stuart-Richardson* [daughter of the 2nd Earl of
Cromartie, married Sir Stewart-Richardson, 15th Baronet, who, as an
officer in the Black Watch, died in 1914 during the First Battle of Ypres]

2. *Simon Flexner* [born in Kentucky, distinguished pathologist, one
of the original Rockefeller Foundation trustees]

3. *Percy Haughton* [he and his wife owned Gould Island in Rhode
Island where he trained the Harvard football team. Two years earlier, in
1916, he purchased the Boston Braves]

4. *August Belmont* [German-American financier, foreign diplomat,
politician, horse-breeder, established the Belmont Stakes and formerly
chaired the Democratic National Committee]

5. *Mary Young Craig – of the Castle Sq.* [Mary Young was an actress.
She met and married John Craig in London when she was thirteen. By
1614, the couple owned and ran the Castle Square Theater in Boston's
South End.]

*Lady Constance always wears a turban and Russian boots in the
morning – sandals and white stockings at night.*

*There is also an amusing Italian aviator – Comte Camilis de
Something who draws Oie Pariesiene* pictures and takes the kidding
everyone gives him with the most wonderful grace.*

*We are all sitting around waiting for tea and Scottie is going to recover
from the flu and come up. He has taught me the most gorgeous British naval
slang – really Bet – he is a gem – hasn't got a cent, and is the homeliest man
God ever made, with the most devine*[sic] *sense of humor. You would love*

him, and so would I, only I won't.

I feel utterly removed from my life over there. I simply can't concentrate my mind on Ted [Baker?] – Tho' you needn't tell him that – I simply forget him for days at a time – and only occasionally past and future reoccur to me as things far away and not important enough to be considered. I can't concentrate on Larry [Noyes?] either – in fact I am afraid my mind is failing utterly and you will come home to find me tucked away in some asylum. In fact about the only thought I have is that I love you and wish you were here — as usual.

Ede Bump.

---

*I think 'Oie Parisiene' means 'Parisian tarts.'

December 19, 1918
[Same day as the previous letter] **RMS Baltic**

This letter was written by the young man in the R.A.F. who Edith
mentioned in the last letter. His handwriting is particularly difficult to
decipher.

S.S. Baltic
Dec 19th 1918

> [Top right corner]
> *Written in a moment of mental strain*
> *by said R.A.F. He ought to know.*

*My Dear Cus+ I am awfully sorry old bean that I haven't mentioned
before now but you know old thing I've met such a wonderful and charming
young British Naval officer and with a rank 1st Lootenant too. Of course
there are also several fine looking British and American Aviators but they
are a bit to[o] flighty for my style of temperament for they seem to be such
serious minded young fellows that I simply cannot fathom them at all.*

*I had a most wonderful experience the other evening. After all the
lights had been turned out in the lounge, one of these R.A.F. boys asked me*

if I would care to study the beauty of our ocean voyage by moonlight. That was my cue for I was crazy to go out there all the time but didn't like to suggest it first. Well I would certainly like to give you the full details of those precious minutes but honestly dear words are indescribable — Oh! It was simply wonderful and when I think that in just two horrid days the trip will be over I could almost cry my eyes out.

Well Dear when I come to think it over and consider my past _[?]_ I cannot realize how I could have possibly been so stimied[sic]. Indeed I have at last come to the conclusion that "The moth should not fly too near the flame."

Good bye my Dear much love from your sorrowfull[sic] but nonetheless __?__ chastised.

Edith

Probably **January 11, 1919**
France

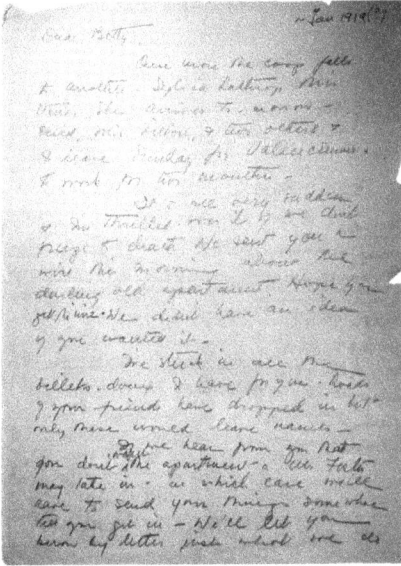

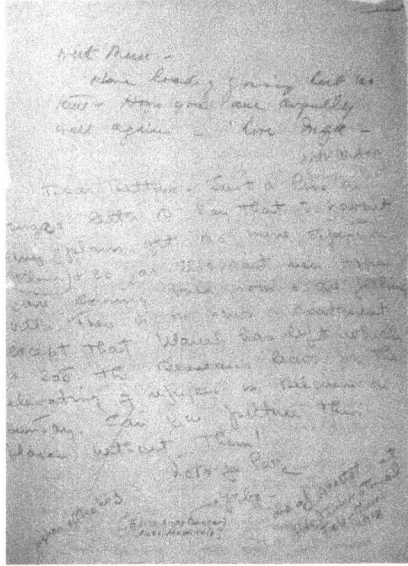

This letter to Betty was not written by Edith, but rather by two of the
three girls Betty lived with in Paris at the Hotel International from
February to March 1918. Betty kept the letter with her collection of
letters from Edith. 'Inga' signed the first part. A second friend, who
wrote in a backhand script, signed with the nickname 'Yebo'.

Marcel, mentioned in the last paragraph, entered Betty's life as "an
orphan office boy," wrote Leila. "His real name was Marcel de la Vaux.
My mother kept in touch with him after the war. In September of 1937,
when she and my father took my sister and me to Paris, we visited Marcel
and his family."

---

11 January 1919

Dear Betty

*Once more the coop falls to another — Sylvia Lathrop this time. She
arrives to-morrow — Enid, Miss Dillon, & two others & I leave Sunday for
Valenciennes – to work for two months.*

*It's all very sudden & I'm thrilled over it if we don't freeze to death. We
sent you a wire this morning about my darling old apartment. Hope you got*

the wire. We didn't have an idea if you wanted it.

I've stuck in all my billets – deux [two] *I have for you – Loads of your friends have dropped in but only these would leave names.*

If we hear from you that you don't want the apartment – a Mr. Fister may take it – in which case you'll have to send your things somewhere 'till you get in – We'll let you know by letter just what we do with them —

Have loads of gossip but no time – Hope you are awfully well again. – Love Inga

On the backside

Dear Bettina – Just a line on Inga's letter to say that I haven't any plans yet as mine [_?_] on Blens[sp?] & 80 jar elle sait reine [she knows nothing]. Hope you're coming back soon & are feeling better. There is no news or excitement except that Marcel has left, which is sad. The Desseaus leave for the elevating of refugees in Belgium on Sunday. Can you picture this place without them!

Lots of love
Yebo

∽∞∞∽

Before we move on to Edith and Betty's lives post World War I, we need to insert an important event that Edith did not mention. In 1919 the French government awarded to Betty's father, Charles Wilberforce, the title of Chevalier de la Legion d'Honneur, France's most important commendation. It was in recognition of the large share he took in relieving the French war sufferers. M. Marcel Knecht conferred the award upon Charles Wilberforce at a large public gathering in St. Paul.*

---

*From the obituary of Charles Wilberforce Ames by Arthur Sweeney: https://archive.org/stream/jstor-20160382/20160382_djvu.txt

Knowlton Lyman Ames, Jr and Edith Ames Winter

Minneapolis and Chicago

We have finally reached the period when my Grandmother Edith first mentioned my grandfather Knowlton Lyman Ames, Jr, of Chicago, Illinois. I have always known they met while in France during WWI. Unfortunately she did not describe how. Along with most of his friends and family, Edith called him 'Junior.' I never met this grandfather even though he didn't die until the same year Edith died, 1965, when I was fourteen. The copy of a painting shown above is the only image I have of him as a young man. The dark photograph of Edith was probably taken during the same period.

January 30, 1919
Minneapolis, Minnesota

Edith is home in Minneapolis. Betty is still in France. Edith's parents, Alice and Thomas Winter, have moved to 2617 Dean Parkway in a suburb on the outer edges of Minneapolis by the Lake of the Isles. The GoogleMaps below shows its relation to the previous home at 418 Groveland Avenue. Today, 418 Groveland houses a law firm in a commercial area.

The following image of the house is also from GoogleMaps.

2617 Dean Blvd.
Minneapolis, Minn.
January 30th [1919]

Betsy darling,
I was so glad to get a letter from you at last and to hear first hand about all the excitement. It makes me a bit sick to think of missing it all, but you had such a rotten time that you are entitled to all the fun you can get and I am glad that it is coming your way. It certainly is a comparison to the quiet life as lived in Minneapolis, but, though I am not doing a thing, and haven't done a lick of work since I came home, I am having about the most contented time I ever knew, and I don't seem to worry about what I am going to do next, or to care, so long as it is as pleasant as the little things that I am finding to do these days. For instance today I went to the meeting of the Study Club in the morning, had lunch with Ellen Hallowell, whose baby is coming in April, and then went out to the other end of nowhere to a meeting of a little club of mothers of soldiers who had begged me to come out and talk to them, the first speach[sic] I have consented to give. Tomorrow Betty Washburn is coming to lunch and we are going skating.

The chief excitement to the week is of course the announcement of Ruf's and Chick's engagement. Everybody was surprised to death and they are all a bit anxious to see how I take it. Luckily it struck me funny and I could do nothing but giggle the first day. Then Lena decided that I had thrown him over, and is, I am sure, making up some very good story about it. Also they have somehow got wind of Ted [Baker] and spend all their time trying to pump me. Ted cabled the other day that he expected to land about February 3rd, and as I am going down to Chicago the end of the month I shall probably see him then. I hope Chuck will be there too. I got a simply darling letter from him today, and he expected to be on his way soon, so here's hoping. Meanwhile Junior writes to be a sport and wait till he gets out of Germany, and Franc Altman expects to be up from Texas within a week or so, and I feel rather as if the world were too much with me. Mr Brown took me to lunch when I was in Chicago last week, and he was simply darling, and sent me a huge bunch of orchids and asked me to go out to Lake Forest for the week, but I promised to do it when I came down to see Ed Baker's family not knowing that Ted would be there then.

Your News about Bill and Inga nearly knocked me flat – I simply can't picture it. Mrs. Dean tried to get the news out of me the other day, and your family wanted to hear all about your beaux, but I think you had better do all that telling yourself. We are all going down there tomorrow night to dinner and the little theater plays, in one of which Alice [Betty's sister] and Epes [Betty's brother-in-law] have parts. The babies are too adorable! I hate to let them out of my sight when I am down there, but now they have moved back to their own house. Joe Mckibbin [Princeton, St. Paul] has gone to New York to live, which is a bitter blow. I had one wonderful party with him the night before I went to Chicago, but when he called up to say goodbye I wasn't here, alas. Sid Strong has gone into business in Seattle, and Skip [Arthur] Hartwell has set off around the world, so you see there isn't so much to play with as there might be and all the rest seem to be married.

So you see there isn't much that I can tell you. When you come home, if you can, will you bring me a couple of jars of Crème de la Reine as my supply is getting low. And lordy, but this child will be glad to see you. You are the only person I can really talk to. Please give my best love to the Dessaus and the Farewells, and Mrs. Lathrop and Miss Vail, and kiss Willie on the brow. And if you see any of my old pals give them my very best. I saw Mrs. Ryerson in Chicago and got some of the dope from her. Mme de Bellize writes that Parish got a Croix de Guerre. My Lord! Please give my love to darling Dolly Watts, and to Agnes. Then when you have done all that you can come home. I am going to move down to your house for a week when you get here.

More love than there is in the world.

Ede

January or February 1919
Hotel Des Anglais & Ruhl, Nice

This letter is from Betty to Edith. Betty is still in France.

Dearest Ede –

How I long for you – this separation is intolerable for we'll never get caught up and I know that besides my six weeks heavenly jaunt on the Riviera to tell you about before I get home there will be a bushel more truck [gossip] to tell you about — and as for what you have to tell me – whew! – Well about the 20th of March [1919], perhaps earlier, I expect to be pulling in to the ole Union Depot at St. Paul – I'm absolutely nutty – I like so many people that I just don't know what I'll ever do – except live long and stoutly an old maid. – I've had a marvelous rest cure down here filled with corking people – the three most important being Bill Spencer, Ken Simpson and Ted Lane* – Bill was just here for a week – and a great one it was, flowers every day, long walks, picnics, motor rides, dinners every sort of delightful time – and we're the best of friends – he's not in love with me nor I with him and its all fine. – Somehow every day I think a bit more about a certain A.W. whom I'm beginning to realize is a very wonderful person but who can tell? He may not care for me.

---

*Leila noted that her mother, Betty, met Ted Lane in France.

'A.W.' was probably Alan Winslow, the aviator who wrote to the young women from the German prison camp asking for clothes and cigarettes.

Kitty commented, "I think my mother was in love with someone in the air squadron who died during the war. Every time the war was mentioned she burst into tears."

Leila, who is older than Kitty, filled in, "Our mother was in love with Warren Hobbs. He was killed over Belgium. It happened quite soon after Betty and Edith moved into the apartment at 3, rue Verde in April 1918. Mother kept in touch with his sister for several years, maybe more, after the war."

Feb 13, 1919

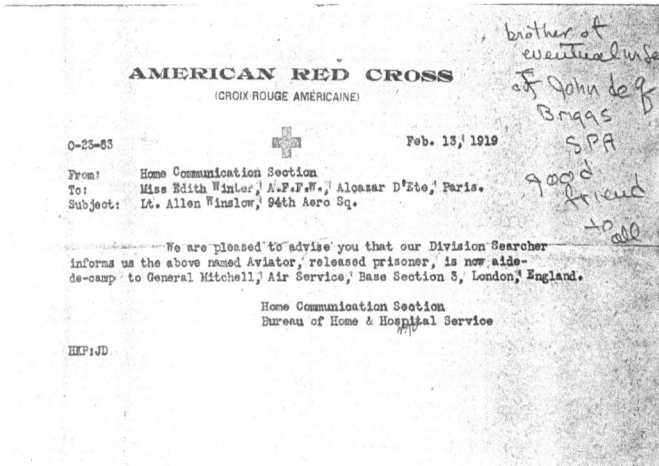

Betty may have forwarded this message to Edith with the letter above. It was addressed to the Alcazar after Edith had returned to Minnesota.

———————

AMERICAN RED CROSS
(CROIX-ROUGE AMÉRICAINE)

0-23-83

Feb. 13, 1919

From: Home Communication Section
To: Miss Edith Winter, A.F.F.W., Alcazar D'Ete, Paris
Subject: Lt. Allen Winslow, 94th Aero Sq.

We are pleased to advise you that our Division Searcher informed us the above named Aviator, released prisoner, is now aide-de-comp to General Mitchell, Air Service, Base Section 3, London, England.

Home Communication Section
Bureau of Home & Hospital Service
HMP:JD

March 18, 1919
Minneapolis, Minnesota

2617 Dean Boulevard,
March 18 [1919]

Betsy dear:-

*You are right, my initials are going to be E.W.A. [Edith Winter Ames].
Now how about you. Junior and I are going to announce our engagement
about the 22nd or 30th. I wanted you to be the first person to know, but
your landing date made that practically impossible, so I have told your
family and written grandma [Fanny Baker Ames in Boston] and Ted
[Baker - no relation to Fanny].*

*I know you don't think Jr is going to make me a good husband, but my
dear, if you could only know how wonderful he is, and he has been to me,
for I have had a horrible time, and Junior has been so wonderfully helpful
and kind and generous through the whole thing.*

*Before you arrange to see Ted [Baker] in Chicago, I ought to tell you
that when I first came home I honestly thought I was in love with him, and
was engaged to him for two weeks. Of course it has been horrible for him
and I never was so sorry for anyone in my life. But when I found out I really
couldn't get on without Junior there was nothing for me to do but break my
engagement and it was particularly awful because Ted's family had been so
wonderful to me.*

*His address is Green Bay Road, Lake Forest, Ill. Chuck's is 821 Forest
Avenue, Evanston.*

Junior is too wonderful to me, Betty. I haven't seen him yet, but he telephoned as soon as he landed, and now he calls up from Chicago once or twice a day, and last night came a big box of pink roses and a corsage of orchids and lilies of the valley. He is coming up on tonight's train and I am afraid we are going to be as big idiots as most engaged people. I certainly never expected to see Junior in the state he is in. I think you will get to like him a lot and I certainly hope you will carry out your threat of frequent visits to Chicago, if we live there – for I haven't an idea where we are going to live or what we are going to do.

Oh Betty, I'm so glad you are at home, and you must stay single long enough to be my maid-of-honor.

Best love,
Edith

———————

Kitty commented, "Mummy didn't approve of Junior when Edith married him. She was always very fair about people. She gave people the benefit of the doubt. But she had her opinions [and her opinion about Junior was not good].

———⟨◊◊◊⟩———

When I was growing up, I did not understand the connections between my different Ames families. It was purely coincidence that Edith married someone with the same last name as her maternal grandfather and became Edith Ames Winter Ames. The two Ames lines are not the same. My grandfather's surname 'Ames' was originally spelled 'Eames' and changed to 'Ames' in 1812. When I researched my grandmother's Ames line, I found that her grandfather Charles Gordon Ames had been adopted by Thomas and Lucy Ames and biologically was not an Ames at all.

Charles Gordon Ames' birth mother was Lucy Knox Thatcher Leeson (1807-1863), the granddaughter of Major General Henry Knox (1750-1806), known for his participation in the Revolutionary War. Lucy became pregnant with Charles out of wedlock and gave him up for adoption. Charles learned of this when he was fourteen. When he was twenty-one, he rode by horseback to the home where Lucy, her husband and their legitimate daughter lived. Only when Lucy's husband left the room did she give Charles the recognition that he sought. With her hand on his, she said, "I know who you are, but my husband must never know." Charles was unable to learn who his father was. After Lucy's death, he tried to pry the name from the Knox family, but they refused to release it. Hence we may never know what his real surname was.

My great-grandfather and grandfather's first name 'Knowlton' came from another Revolutionary War ancestor. Lieutenant Thomas Knowlton (1740-1776) was shot and killed while leading his Knowlton's Rangers against the British in the Battle of Harlem Heights – a battle the Patriots won.

The middle name 'Lyman' came from our ancestor Lyman Rose of Ohio (1817-1901). Coincidently, or maybe not, Lyman was also the surname of Betty's maternal grandmother, Susan Inches Lyman Lesley (1823-1904).

June 2, 1919
Chicago, Illinois

The return address on this letter is for the home of Junior's parents, Knowlton Lyman Ames, Sr (1868-1931), and Adelaide Schroeder Ames (1870-1948). Knowlton, Edith's future father-in-law, was dubbed with the nickname 'Snake' when he played football for Princeton University, where he graduated in 1890. The name referred to the way he writhed through the opposing team. He played so well he was inducted in the College Football Hall of Fame. He was also credited for developing the 'drop kick.'

By 1919, Snake was president of a business conglomerate called Booth Fisheries that owned the *Chicago Journal of Commerce* newspaper. He served as the *Journal*'s CEO. Later, in the early 1950s, the *Journal* was sold by my grandfather's brother, John Ames, to the *Wall Street Journal*.

Edith's mother-in-law-to-be, Adelaide, was born and raised in Brooklyn, New York, where her father, Frederick Anthony Schroeder (1833-1899), had served as mayor from 1875 to 1877, the year the first wire was strung for the Brooklyn Bridge. His name is on a plaque repeated on both towers.

Adelaide's father was an example of the American Dream come true. He migrated to America from Trier, Germany, in 1848 or 1849 at age fifteen or sixteen with little more than change in his pocket. He also had some knowledge of cigar making. For a while Frederick sold cigars on New York City's street corners. After developing a new way to roll cigars, he started his own manufacturing company, Schroeder & Bon.

Eventually, he owned a home in Brooklyn, the property for which, wrote his granddaughter Rosemary (Junior's little sister), "took up the whole block." Frederick Schroeder's success allowed him to help found the Germania Savings Bank. He served as a New York state senator from 1880 to 1881. He died in 1899 some seventeen years before Edith and Junior met.

When Edith's in-laws-to-be, Snake and Adelaide, got married in Brooklyn back in 1893, a thousand guests attended. However, by the time Edith moved in with them in 1919, things were not going well. A year after Edith and Junior's marriage, in 1920, Snake will divorce Adelaide to be with his mistress, Ada Howell, who he will marry in 1922. They will have a baby in 1926 named Emily Ames – a half sister-in-law to Edith.

Junior already had a younger brother named John and a beautiful red-headed sister named Rosemary – the Rosemary I just mentioned. In the 1930's, Rosemary will move to Hollywood, become an actress, and in 1935 play the role of Shirley Temple's mother in the movie, *Our Little Girl*.

But at the time Edith moved in with the Ames family in Chicago, John was only sixteen and Rosemary was thirteen.

Junior had followed his father's example and attended Princeton University. Also like his father, he played football. Knowlton Lyman Ames Jr. was not as famous as Knowlton Lyman Ames, Sr, but he was credited with making the first touchdown in Palmer Stadium. Junior graduated in 1917 right before joining the service in France. One article said he was six feet four inches tall. His sister, Rosemary, called him a "ladies man."

Edith had moved into a household accustomed to drama. The drama will increase.

---

936 Lake Shore Drive
June 2nd

Dearest Betts :–

I won't be back until the end of the week. So I am going to ask you to do something I should have attended to long ago. We want some music for the night of the bridal dinner – Wednesday the 25th – from about eight till one I guess – and four or five pieces. I would rather have Dryor if we can get him – if not – Shilbey. Will you try and reserve one or the other of these for that night. It is a dirty trick to wish this job of mine on you but you are such a lamb I know you won't mind.

My in-laws are altogether too wonderful to me and we are having the best time – parties, looking for apartments which apparently don't exist, and getting furniture. We got the most wonderful dining room set of dark mahogany – There is a table, round only squared off at the edges like this [sketch of a circle]. *Then there is a long narrow side board, a serving table, a cupboard, six straight chairs and an arm chair. It is the lovliest*[sic] *set. Jr. and I both agreed on it the moment we saw it, and grabbed it right away. This afternoon we are going to look at an apartment which sounds very promising – three bathrooms – which is my idea of heaven.*

I met your friend Hash Gile* the other day. He came over and sat down at our table at the Blackstone and I almost fell on his neck. They gave a dinner before the dance at the Opera Club the other night and Alan Winslow and Sam Farrington came. Alan is wonderful, dances, drives the machine, ties his ties and shoes, and seems perfectly normal [even though he has only one arm]. *It is hot as the dickens and I have the curse but those are my only troubles in the world. I get crazies about Jr. every time I look at him. So I will soon be in an awful state.*

Best love dear, and apologies for bothering you about the music.
Edith.

---

*Leila added that Hash Tile was part of her father Norris Jackson's Princeton crowd. She also noted that Alan Winslow's sister Margery (Mrs. John de Briggs), became the headmaster of St. Paul Academy which Betty's father and father-in-law had helped found. "Mrs Brigges kept the position for decades."

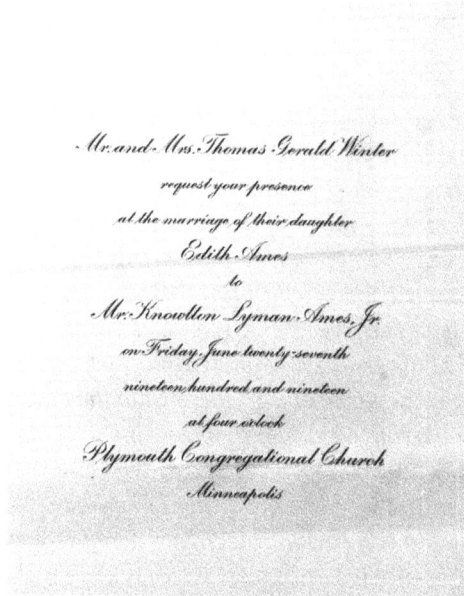

Mr. and Mrs. Thomas Gerald Winter
request your presence
at the marriage of their daughter
Edith Ames
to
Mr. Knowlton Lyman Ames, Jr.
on Friday, June twenty-seventh
nineteen hundred and nineteen
at four o'clock
Plymouth Congregational Church
Minneapolis

Junior was twenty-five and Edith twenty-three on their wedding day. [She was the same age I was on my wedding day.] My Uncle Bud sent me this faded photo-copy of a news article from a Minneapolis newspaper.

Betty saved articles from the *Minneapolis Journal* and *The St. Paul*. I found the Witness Book in my dad's collection. Thirty-five people signed, even though a newspaper headline read, "Hundreds at Ceremony." Elizabeth Ames is at the very top of the list. Her future husband, Norris Dean Jackson, signed farther down.

One article announced:

"One of the most fashionable weddings of the season, the culmination of a war romance, took place this afternoon when Miss Edith Winter, daughter of Mr. and Mrs. Thomas G. Winter, became the bride of Knowlton Lyman Ames, Jr. son of Mrs. and Mrs. Knowlton Lyman Ames of Chicago. The wedding was the culmination of a romance that had its inception during the days of "Flanders' Field" and the shelltorn and bombarded regions near Paris, when Mr. Ames, then a lieutenant in the U.S. Army, and his bride, who had volunteered for overseas service under the American Fund for French Wounded, met. Mr. Ames was stationed at one time at the Anti-aircraft school at Bonesse, a member of the 122nd Field Artillery. After the signing of the armistice, he acted as an aide to Lieutenant Colonel Searle Harries of the U.S.M.R.C.

"In an attractive setting of white peonies, white lilacs, ferns and lighted cathedral candles the ceremony was performed at 4 o'clock by Rev. Harry P. Dewy in the presence of a large number of friends and relatives of the bride and bridegroom. Hamlin Hunt at the organ, played a program of nuptial music before and during the ceremony.

"The bridal party entered to the strains of the 'Bridal Chorus' from Wagner's 'Lohengrin.' The ushers were the first to enter. They included William H. Schoen, Jr. of Pittsburgh; Ackert Banks of Chicago; Amory Haskell of New York City, Theodore B. Keating of Buffalo, N.Y., Wilfred Anderson of Chicago, Theodore G. Ames of St. Paul, a cousin of the bride and Alan Winslow of Chicago. Mr. Winslow was the first American aviator to bring down a German plane following the entry of the United States in the war. He was seriously wounded losing his left arm in an aerial battle and for four months was in a German prison camp.

"Miss Betty Ames of St. Paul, a cousin of the bride, was the maid of honor and preceded the bride. She wore a dainty gown of lavender organdie fashioned with short sleeves, a vest of lace and a belt of lavender moire ribbon. The skirt was finished at the bottom with an escalloped edge. Miss Ames wore a hat of lavender, tulle trimmed with daisies and dahlias and carried an arm bouquet of pink roses.

"The six other attendants including Mrs. Morris Hallowell Jr., and the Misses Margaret Fogue, Ruth Eggleston, Eleanor Dewey, and Florence and Cora Stevenson, wore gowns similar to Miss Ames' in pink organdie with lavender ribbon sashes and hats of pink tulle. Their flowers were pink roses in arm bouquets.

"The bride, who entered with her father, was met at the altar by Mr. Ames and his best man, J.P. Scully of New York. The bridal gown was an attractive model of white satin elaborated in lace. The skirt was cut round length and the bodice of satin had a vest of Venetian lace and long sleeves of georgette crepe. A court train of satin fell from the shoulders. The long veil was of point de esprit and trimmed in Belgian lace. The bride carried a shower bouquet of orange blossoms, lilies of the valley and orchids.

"Mrs. Winter, the bride's mother wore blue georgette with trimmings of white lace and a Milan straw hat with flower trimmings. She had a corsage bouquet of orchids. Mrs Ames, the bridegroom's mother, wore gray and had a corsage of orchids.

"Being a victory and peace month bride, Miss Winter had gone back, as almost all brides, to the pretty postwar wedding customs. Only the national colors and those of preferred Allied nations today remind of the years of war.

"Following the ceremony a reception was held at the home of the bride's parents, 2617 Dean boulevard for the intimate friends and relatives. Receiving with the bride and bridegroom were Mr. and Mrs. Winter, parents of the bride, and Mr. and Mrs. Ames, the bridegroom's parents. Garden flowers in large vases and wall pockets were used throughout the house.

"Mr. Ames and his bride will leave tonight on an extended wedding trip to the Canadian Rockies and Honolulu. [They will get no farther than San Francisco.] Upon their return they will be at home at 61 Elm St., Chicago.

"Mr. and Mrs. Ames and their daughter, Miss Rosemary Ames arrived this noon from Chicago in a special car with a group of Chicago people including Mr. and Mrs. C.A. Banis, Mr. and Mrs. H. Holtz, Mr. and Mrs. A.F. Banks, Mr. and Mrs. William Dawes and Mr. and Mrs. Martin. They will return to Chicago late this evening. Mrs. Charles G. Ames [Fanny Baker Ames] of Boston, grandmother of the bride, and Mrs. George J. Allen of Rochester, Minn., were other out of town guests.

"Miss Elizabeth Ames, the maid of honor, shared in the overseas volunteer work of the bride."

Betty saved the above article showing the cousins. It mentions how in the selection of the marriage date, "the bride had been guided by sentiment, for the last week in June has always been a 'wedding week' in the Winter family." Edith's parents (Alice and Thomas Winter), Edith's grandparents (Charles Gordon Ames and Fanny Baker) and Edith's aunt (Edith Theodora Ames and Raymond Cosby) had all been married on June 25. But Rev. Dewey of Plymouth Church was not available that day. [My daughter, Amy Claire McCormick, now Amy Claire Vokey, who is Edith's great-granddaughter, got married on June 25 in 2011.]

The article stated that the choice of the Canadian Rockies, "one of the famous scenic beauty spots in the world" also guided plans for the wedding trip because it was the scene of the first meeting of Mr. and Mrs. Winter. Alice met Thomas while on a train. Alice had been in Yellowstone with her brother Charles Wilberforce and the train stopped in Banff in the Canadian Rockies on its way back to Minnesota. Family lore states it was "love at first sight."

Much of Edith's wedding ensemble had family history:

"A vest of lace on the bodice was made of old rose point, an heirloom in the bride's family, which had been worn by her great-grandmother on her wedding day ...

"The full length court train that hung square from a fold of charmeuse, also had its family associations for it had been worn by three brides in the family, the cousins of Miss Winter: Mrs. Samuel E. Turner (Catharine), Mrs. Cushing F. Wright (Margaret), and Mrs. Bronson Crothers (Alice), all of St. Paul, as had the veil of beautiful old Honiton lace, which hung in a deep point to the hem of the train ... becomingly fastened with orange blossoms.

"The night before the wedding, Elizabeth gave a bridal supper for her cousin and Mr. Ames ... at her home, 501 Grand Ave, entertaining 60 guests. After the buffet supper the party went to the University club dance."

The article published with the photo below, also saved by Betty, added that after Junior's parents arrived in their private train car, they "took apartments at the Hotel Plaza," where a luncheon was given in their honor. The Chicago guest list included Junior's sister, Rosemary; Snake and Adelaide's son, John; Mr. and Mrs. Walter W. Ross and their sons: Walter Willard Jr, Ames Ross Robert Ross; Mr. William Dawes; and Miss Emily McCormick of Evanston. Except for Junior's brother and sister, these people were cousins.

Leila noted that the Honiton lace wedding veil, originally purchased for Betty's sister Catharine, "is still in the Charles W. Ames family."

Wedding of Miss Edith Winter
and Mr. Knowlton L. Ames, Jr.,
Culmination of War Romance

PHOTO BY SWEET

Mrs Knowlton Lyman Ames Jr

August 5, 1919
Chicago, Illinois

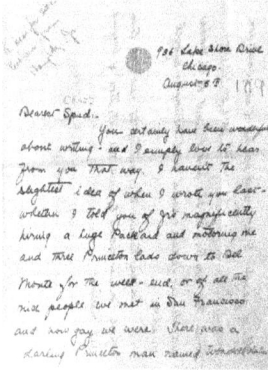

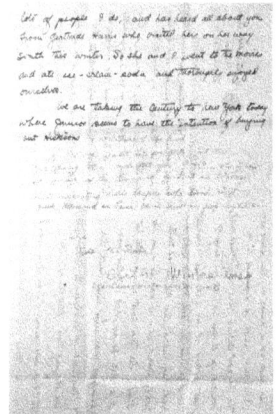

Edith wrote this letter a month and a half after her wedding. Even though the wedding articles stated that she and Junior were going to take up residence at 61 Elm Street, Edith still writes on EAW monogrammed stationery and the couple is still living with Junior's parents.

Soldiers returning en masse from the war caused a housing shortage. According to my parents, the same thing happened after World War II ended.

---

936 Lake Shore Drive Chicago.
August 5th

Dearest Spud:–

You certainly have been wonderful about writing – and I simply love to hear from you that way. I haven't the slightest idea of when I wrote you last – whether I told you of Jr's magnificently hiring a huge Packard and motoring me and three Princeton lads down to Del Monte for the weekend, or of all the nice people we met in San Francisco and how gay we were. There was a darling Princeton man named Wendell Kubee[sp?] who gave us a dinner at their place at Burlingame which is supposed to be the Newport suburb, and when the French maid bounced up to help us with our things I just looked at her and said "Comment", as if it were the only French word I had ever heard. Then the English butler nearly floored me – he was so much like Oliver. The trip east was horribly hot and dirty so my first act here was *shampoo, manicure and bath. Mr. & Mrs. Aliver/Winer[?] of Jacksonville (silver pitcher) are staying here. Mrs. Ames & the children* [John and Rosemary] *are away. Mrs. Aliver/Winer[?] was in Kay Macs class at Spence* [a school in New York City]* *and knows lots of people I do, and has heard all about you from Gertrude Harris* [a special childhood friend of Betty's from St. Paul known as 'Trudy'] *who visited her on her way south this winter. So she and I went to the movies and ate ice-cream-soda and thoroughly enjoyed ourselves.*

[Writing from the train] *We are taking the* [Twentieth] *Century* [Limited]** *to New York today where Junior seems to have the intention of buying out Hicksons or something of the kind.*

*We are almost into New York, but there is one fiery item I must tell you – Guess who I saw at dinner at the Bismarck Gardens**** in Chicago*[?] *That disgusting little chapier who lived with Dick Hennard*[sp?] *in Paris. He is just as pop-eyed as ever.*

Love
Ede-the Swede

––––––––––

*The "Spence School" is in New York City at 22 East 91st Street.

**My Uncle Bud, who grew up in Chicago – whereas my father grew up in California – spoke about the *Twentieth Century Limited* train with great pride. According to Wikipedia, the train line was inaugurated on June 17, 1902, ten years before Edith wrote this letter. "[The *Twentieth Century Limited* was] an express passenger train operated by the New York Central Railroad until 1967, during which time it would become known as the 'National Institution' and the 'Most Famous Train in the World.'

"The train traveled between Grand Central Terminal in New York City and La Salle Street Station Chicago, Illinois, along the railroad's 'Water Level Route.' It was in direct competition to the Pennsylvania Railroad aimed at upper class as well as business travelers. Originally the trip took 20 hours. In 1905 it took 18 hours. After another train wreck in Ohio, it reverted to 20 hours. The schedule remained unchanged until 1932.

"[The *Century*] departed New York City westbound in the evening and arrived LaSalle St. Station the following morning. The fare in the 1920s was $32.70 plus the extra fare of $9.60, plus the Pullman charge (e.g. $9 for a lower berth), for a total of $51.30, equal to $680 today. For that, one received a bed closed off from the aisle by curtains; a compartment to oneself would have cost much more."

Imagine how much Snake and Adelaide Ames paid for the private train car that took them from Chicago to Minneapolis for Junior and Edith's wedding.

In 1928 the *Century* was believed to be the most profitable train in the world. "Streamlined in 1939, passengers walked to and from the cars on a plush, crimson carpet which was rolled out in New York and Chicago and was specially designed for that train – hence the term, red carpet treatment."

***A Bismark Hotel is still located across the street from Chicago's City Hall. The original was built in 1894. Five years after Edith's letter, in 1926, the hotel was razed and remodeled.

October, 1919

Image source: http://www.authentichistory.com/1898-1913/2-progressivism/7-prohibition/19190125_American_Issue.jpg

No where in this collection of letters does Edith mention that by October of 1919, the creation, possession, selling, buying, and consumption of alcohol was outlawed in the United States.

Novelist F. Scott Fitzgerald's book, *The Great Gatsby*, published six years later, described the society that my grandparents experienced during Prohibition, both in the Midwest and on the East Coast. Edith and Junior's lives paralleled Fitzgerald's life in many ways. Fitzgerald was born in St. Paul in 1896, the year after Edith was born across the river in Minneapolis in 1895. As mentioned, Fitzgerald attended St. Paul Academy, the boys country day school that Betty's brothers and future husband attended – the same school Betty's father and future father-in-law helped found. Fitzgerald attended Princeton with both Betty's future husband and Edith's future husband. He was friends with Norris, but not with Junior.

Leila commented, "Daddy and Don Bigelow [who Edith mentioned in an earlier letter] had to, on many occasions, put Scott to bed after one of his drinking binges. Fitzgerald took dancing classes with my Uncle Teddy, and supposedly, he based his character 'the observer' in *The Great Gatsby* off of my father."

Fitzgerald dropped out of Princeton in 1917 to join the Army the year Junior and Norris graduated. Fitzgerald's family made their fortune in Minnesota as grocers, while Edith's father, Thomas Winter, ran grain elevators. Junior's father owned a newspaper, while Scott Fitzgerald wrote for newspapers.

A big difference was that Scott Fitzgerald's parents were Catholics. The Winters were strict Presbyterians and the Ameses were Unitarians. Fitzgerald did not travel to France until after World War I, in 1926.

The parallel I find most fascinating is that from the time Scott Fitzgerald, Edith Winter, and Knowlton Lyman Ames Jr. left their Ivy League schools, to when they turned forty, Prohibition was in full force. Yet, all three young adults seem to have spent the majority of their leisure time partying and drinking.

February 10, 1920
Chicago, Illinois

The envelope for this letter was addressed to Betty c/o R.M. Crosby, Yarmouthport Massachusetts, then forwarded to "Turner, 14 Francis Ave, Cambridge, MA." Betty was visiting Aunt E and her husband Raymond.

---

21 East Elm Street
Chicago
February 10th

Dearest Betsy:–
You were a dear to write me such a nice letter from Gertrude's* and I meant to answer it ages ago and tell you how I adored even the little glimpse I had of you. But I just don't seem to do anything.
Let's see what has happened. Last week we were quite gay in the mild way of having two people at a time to dinner. Mother arrived Thursday night and will be here two weeks going to various meetings, which is perfectly great because Jr. has to go off again for a five day trip on Thursday. She isn't very well – left home with a fever and bad throat but she has been loafing by the fire for three days and is much better. Today I went apartment hunting with little Farwell-Stevenson, in vain. It has come to the point where you go and ring door-bells and ask the janitor if there is apt to be anything to rent within a few months. Then they say "no" and slam the door. Poor Helen is getting desperate. We ended at Mrs. Kent Chandlers to see her husky new son and then the three of us had tea and toast and

conversation at Helen's.

I have had a relapse these last-few days and have been feeling just like the dickens – so I have been sticking pretty near home. Chuck came in Sunday night and was as nice as ever. He brought a man who is working for C.E. Brown, Sr, and insisted on talking about Ted and Betty till we were all nearly in hysterics. They (Ted and Betty) have sublet an apartment at 31 East Elm – the entry with Martha dow[?] Douglas – so he must feel quite at home. I really think it is awfully funny.

Paul Nelson is going back next month for 4 years of architecture at the Beaux Arts – or rather to loaf away four years in Paris – However, I shall get him to send me some of my pet perfume.

I went apartment hunting with Helen Stevenson. I told you that didn't I – Well there really is no news at all so I shall just send you, and all the Yarmouth family, much love, and let it go at that.

The love.

[An arrow leads to a sketch of some lips.]

Edith

---

*Leila added that Gertrude 'Trudy' Harris later married John Harder.

February 11, 1920

WEDNESDAY, FEBRUARY 11, 1920.

WINTER POSTERS FEATURE MEETING

Women's Club Federation Boosts Minneapolis Woman at Mid-year Convention.

Winter outside and inside. If there wasn't a covering of snow on the ground which naturally serves as a reminder of winter, it couldn't escape one's attention after once entering the Y. W. C. A., where the midwinter meeting of the Minnesota Federation of Women's Clubs opened its two-days' session at 9:30 A. M. today. There are posters boosting "Winter" hung everywhere, not for King Boreas, but for Mrs. Thomas G. Winter of Minneapolis, Minnesota's candidate for prsident of the General Federation of Women's Clubs, which meets in biennial session in Des Moines in June.

"We'll put the 'win' in Winter," was selected as the prize slogan.

Women from all sections of the state were arriving all morning. The day's program was begun with a conference of district presidents from 9:30 to 10:30 A. M. Simultaneously conferences were held by the various standing committees.

At 10:30 A. M. the district presidents, club presidents and state committee chairmen assembled in the auditorium. The program was opened by an address by Dr. L. J. Matos of New York City, who is conducting a dye exhibit at the Golden Rule under the auspices of the National Aniline and Chemical company.

The formal opening of the session was held at 1:30 P. M., when the general delegation met to hear the mid-winter reports.

Miss Lucille Halladay of Minneapolis opened the afternoon session with community singing. The speakers of the afternoon included Mrs. Amy Robbins Ware of Robbinsdale, who gave "Echoes from France," and Leo Gessell, Hamline Y. W. C. A., who spoke on "Community Work for Boys."

It was announced at the meeting today that a campaign committee of fifty women has been formed in Chicago to boost for Mrs. Winter's candidacy.

Four hundred club women of Chicago will entertain Mrs. Winter at a luncheon tomorrow noon at the Woman's club, Chicago.

Tomorrow marks the annual mid-winter breakfast to be given at 1 P. M. in the Palm room at The Saint Paul, preceding which an informal reception will be held in one of the parlors.

Mrs. Guy Maxwell of Winona acted as presiding officer, in the absence of Mrs. George Allen of Rochester, president.

Mrs. J. E. Rounds, president of the Fourth district, will be hostess to members of the executive board at a 6:30 P. M. dinner today at the Athletic club.

In the previous letter, Edith mentioned that her mother, Alice Winter (formally known as Mrs. T.G. Winter) was in Chicago attending meetings. The meetings were about her candidacy for president of the General Federation of Women's Clubs that oversaw philanthropic women's organizations around the country such as the Junior League. The Federation was scheduled to hold its biennial meeting and elections in June. Betty saved the above news article published the day after Edith's letter.

In summary, it stated that the Minneapolis chapter of the Federation had opened a two day session of its midwinter meeting at the Minneapolis Y.W.C.A. (Young Women's Christian Association). As the headline intimated, posters hung about the place claiming "We will put the win in Winter" boosting Alice's candidacy. In addition, a campaign committee of fifty Chicago women had been formed who were organizing a lunch for four hundred club women in Alice's honor in Chicago the following day.

April 3, 1920
Chicago, Illinois

According to Leila, Edith sent this letter to the Queen's Park Hotel in Trinidad in the West Indies where Betty had traveled with her parents and a friend named Laura. The envelope was postmarked "pm 1920."

Edith is pregnant with her first son, my Uncle Bud, whom she and Junior will name Knowlton Lyman Ames III.

Edith writes on her husband's monogrammed stationery.

———————————

K.L.A. Jr.

21 East Elm St
Chicago
April 3rd.

Dearest Betsy:–

I was so pleased to find your letter waiting when I came back from a week's jaunt to Minneapolis, made while Jr. was off on a business trip. Your trip sounds heavenly – but I am especially interested in your having seen and liked Ted Lane* again. I like the sound of that man.

I got back from my trip yesterday morning; and Jr. got back too and it was too slick to see him again. Today we went up to 'Lucile's' and he got me a very sporty blue cape and hat, so I shall feel grand, if fat, on Easter – and then I stopped in to see Nubbin's, and Yebo was there so I sat and jawed for ages. Yebo is just back from California where she saw a lot of Crafts – dear old Crafts – and of course they both wanted to know the latest news about you. Let's see what gossip I have to tell you – mostly babies. Kay MacMillan in August – Margaret Fogue in October – Dee Viall in August, Sarah Ladd in May. Kay Marfield and Edmund are announcing their engagement tomorrow – isn't it great! The Dessaus are going out

[End of letter - The rest must be lost]

---

*Betty became engaged to Ted Lane but broke it off when she learned he had neglected to tell her about a previous marriage.

November 30, 1921

MRS. WINTER WARNS THE WOMEN AGAINST BEING INDIFFERENT

Should Read Less Fatty Arbuckle and Little More International Relations.

By CONSTANCE DREXEL.

Public Ledger-Duluth Herald Service.
Copyright, 1921, by Public Ledger Co.

Washington, Nov. 30.—Women all over the land who have been yearning for a look at the Washington conference stars would have been satisfied, at least so far as the feminine contingent is concerned, at the huge luncheon meeting staged by the General Federation of Women's Clubs.

The particular occasion was the birthday of the national president, Mrs. Thomas G. Winter, one of the four women advisory delegates to the conference. But when the news was published in the local papers that most of the foreign as well as the American women stars would be honor guests, which means they would sit at a raised table where everybody could see them, every club woman in Washington subscribed to a ticket and the rush filled the banquet hall of the hotel and all the adjoining rooms to overflowing.

* * *

It was just the kind of a luncheon women's organizations get up all over the country, but nowhere else could there have been such an international gathering. After the ice cream and coffee, everybody pulled up their chairs and gathered in front of the long table where the honor guests were seated, not only to hear the speeches, but to get a good look at the women everybody had been reading about in the newspapers.

Right in the center was Mrs. Winter, looking quite regal in a handsome white dress and wearing a jeweled brooch that must have been a birthday present. In spite of the fact she is rushed nearly to death with advisory committee meetings and engagements to speak at meetings, she seems to be standing the strain and was in her usual genial good humor, so familiar to the clubwomen of the land.

* * *

Mrs. Joseph Frizell, president of the district Federation of Women's Clubs, introduced her and, regarding the conference, Mrs. Winter said Secretary Hughes had not only honored the America of the past, but had set the flag a few steps further toward the America of the future. And then, instead of overwhelming the women with compliments about having created the sentiment which had called forth the conference, she warned them against indifference because all the ugly forces that would prevent the conference from succeeding are in action.

Then Mrs. Winter, knowing her audience, did just what they hoped she would do. She pointed to each of the women at the honor table and told their names and who they were. There was Lady Geddes, wife of the British ambassador; Lady Borden, wife of the premier of Canada, who spoke a few words of greeting from the women of Canada; Mrs. Hughes, who smiled and bowed; Madame Sze, wife of the Chinese minister, whom everybody thought perfectly fascinating as she bowed her acknowledgments; other women from the Orient, Madame Samuri, wife of a Japanese advisory delegate; Mlle. Limoges, representing Madame Jusserand; Madame Inouye, another Japanese woman, who has been sent by the Japanese Women's Peace society, and Miss Scanlon, who came from the farthest country of all.

* * *

Miss Scanlon made a great hit with her audience, telling about New Zealand, 10,000 miles away, leading the pace for many other countries in progressive legislation which bore fruits in the lowest death rate and lowest infant death rate of the world. She is here to report the conference for New Zealand newspapers but is the only woman in Washington from New Zealand. She spoke of her astonishment at the way American women were not only backing the men, but leading the way.

Mrs. Winter closed the occasion with another pointed hint at the indifference of women.

"Can't we read a little less Fatty Arbuckle and a little more international relations?" she asked.

This article, also saved by Betty, is the sequel to the article about Edith's mother Alice Winter's bid for president of the Federation of Women's clubs.

Mrs. Winter Warns The Women Against Being Indifferent
Should Read Less Fatty Arbuckle* and Little More International
Relations
By Constance Drexel,
Public Ledger-Duluth *Herald Service*
Copyright, 1921, by Public Ledger Co.

Washington, Nov. 30.— Women all over the land who have been
yearning for a look at the Washington conference stars would have been
satisfied, at least so far as the feminine contingent is concerned, at the
huge luncheon meeting staged by the General Federation of Women's
Clubs.

The particular occasion was the birthday of the national president,
Mrs. Thomas G. Winter, one of the four women advisory delegates of the
conference. But when the news was published in the local papers that
most of the foreign as well as the American women stars would be honor
guests, which means they would sit at a raised table where everybody
could see them, every club woman in Washington subscribed to a ticket
and rushed to fill the banquet hall of the hotel and all the adjoining
rooms to overflowing.

It was just the kind of a luncheon women's organizations get up
all over the country, but nowhere else could there have been such an
international gathering. After the ice cream and coffee, everybody pulled
up their chairs and gathered in front of the long table where the honor
guests were seated, not only to hear the speeches, but to get a good look
at the women everybody had been reading about in the newspapers.

Right in the center was Mrs. Winter, looking quite regal in a
handsome white dress and wearing a jeweled brooch that must have
been a birthday present. In spite of the fact that she is rushed nearly to
death with advisory committee meetings and engagements to speak at
meetings, she seems to be standing the strain and was in her usual genial
good humor, so familiar to the club-women of the land. ...

Then Mrs. Winter, knowing her audience, did just what they hoped
she would do. She pointed to each of the women at the honor table and
told their names and who they were.

There was Lady Geddes wife of the British ambassador; Lady Borden,
wife of the premier of Canada, who spoke a few words of greeting from
the women of Canada; Mrs. Hughes*, who smiled and bowed; Madame
Sze, wife of the Chinese minister, whom everybody thought perfectly
fascinating as she bowed her acknowledgments; other women from the

Orient, Madame Samuri, wife of a Japanese advisory delegate; Mlle. Limoges, representing Madame Jusserand; Madame Inouye, another Japanese woman, who has been sent by the Japanese Women's Peace society and Miss Scanlon, who came from the farthest country of all.

Mrs. Scanlon made a great hit with her audience telling about New Zealand, 10,000 miles away, leading the pace for many other countries in progressive legislation which bore fruits in the lowest death rate and lowest infant death rate of the world. She is here to report the conference for New Zealand newspapers but is the only woman in Washington from New Zealand. She spoke of her astonishment at the way American women were not only backing the men, but leading the way.

Mrs. Winter closed the occasion with another pointed hint at the indifference of women. "Can't we read a little less Fatty Arbuckle and a little more international relations?" she asked.

---

*Fatty Arbuckle (1887-1933), born Roscoe Conkling Arbuckle, was, by 1921, an American comedian, screenwriter, director and one of the highest paid actors in Hollywood. A year earlier, in 1920, he signed a million dollar movie contract (over thirteen million in today's dollars). But just days before the conference for the Federation of Women's Clubs, he was tried for raping and killing actress Virginia Rappe. The trial ended in a hung jury.

*Mrs. Hughes was the wife of Charles Evans Hughes (1861-1948). Wikipedia describes Charles Hughes as "an American statesman, lawyer, and Republican politician from New York. He served as the 36th Governor of New York (1907–1910), Associate Justice of the Supreme Court of the United States (1910–1916), United States Secretary of State (1921–1925), a judge on the Court of International Justice (1928–1930), and the 11th Chief Justice of the United States (1930–1941). He was the Republican nominee in the 1916 U.S. Presidential election, losing narrowly to incumbent President Woodrow Wilson. [That was just the first paragraph about him!]

My father, Tom, Edith's middle son, often said to me that his mother lived in her own mother's shadow. I understand why. A comprehensive list of Alice Ames Winter's accomplishments would double the length of this book and more. I could include the letters written to her by Nobel prize winner Madame Curie, and how Alice helped organize American women to gather the funds for Madame Curie to purchase her own gram of radium. I could include a thank you letter from Jane Addams of the Hull House. I *did* insert the above photo of Alice in Egypt with President Warren G. Harding, which I found with my father's memorabilia. It was not dated. I am also inserting a close up of Alice and her companion.

I mentioned earlier that journalist Lillian E. Taafe interviewed Alice for the feminist magazine *The Woman Citizen* on May 31, 1924. According to the *Encyclopedia Britannica*, "*The Woman Citizen, American weekly periodical* [was] one of the most influential women's publications of the early decades of the 20th century," It was founded in 1917 by merging three suffrage journals: the *Woman's Journal*, the *National Suffrage News*, and *Woman Voter*. Besides reporting on the status of women's suffrage, *The Woman Citizen* reported on child labor. [Remember, Alice's mother, Fanny, was the first woman factory inspector.]

One of Taafe's questions was how Alice balanced her activities with being a wife and mother. Alice responded:

"Woman does not necessarily have to choose [between a career and being a wife, mother, and grandmother]; at least I did not. It is possible to marry and still have a career. And what's more, many men who object to their wives having interests outside the home will be bored to death living with them ten years from now. It is not only possible for a woman to marry and have a career but it is in my mind one of the finest ways of holding a husband, since the woman vitally alive stands a better chance of keeping his interest."

Ms. Taffe asked, "But what is the secret of it? Tell me the formula."

"Well," [Mrs. Winter] responded, "Mr. Winter and I spend our evenings together, and in all the years I have been doing things, until just recently when I have had to be out of the city a great deal, I don't think he ever discovered I was busy. That was because I made a point of never working at night. It was his leisure and I felt I owed it to him to keep my time free then, too.

"But, anyhow, Mr. Winter's attitude toward me and my work has never been one of indulgence; but rather he has held that I had a right to do it if I made good."

Ms. Taffe asked if the death of her son Gilbert had anything to do with joining public life.

"Yes, probably more than any one single incident. I felt I could never bear up under my sorrow and I had to keep my mind occupied constantly with other things. But out of it all a certain sympathy came to me that I probably would not otherwise have had, an understanding of other women. And do you know I have had hundreds come to me in trouble – women who never would if they hadn't – well, felt that I understood."

———————

Alice's position as president of the Federation of Women's Clubs came after a string of other philanthropic positions. She would write two more books, both on the subject of women: *The Business of Being a Club Woman*, published in 1925, [four years after the above article] and *The Heritage of Women*, published in 1927. To Alice, running non-profit organizations was a science.

But what about Edith? Who was paying attention to her?

———————

Edith's father, Thomas Winter, was also busy in 1921. Betty's daughters remember their Uncle Tom. "He was a naturalist," said Kitty.

"In 1921, he joined other civic and business leaders of Minneapolis to help organize Encampment Forest," said Leila. The area was once a logging site from which twenty-four-foot logs were transported to England for building ships. It is still a private club today. "They named the camp after a Scandinavian known as Encampment Anderson."

"It was a place to go where it was woody," said Kitty. "It was near the shores of Lake Superior. The Pillsbury family went there, too."

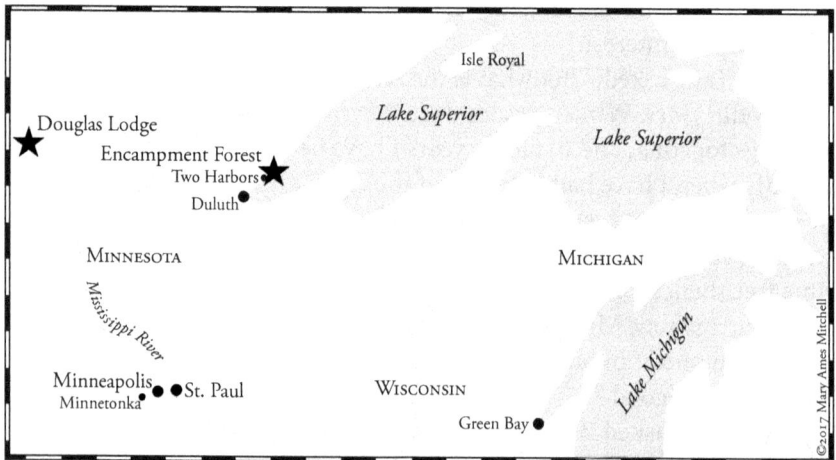

The Walker Art Museum displayed this old post card of the camp's entrance on their website. The photograph is sub-titled: "Where you leave dull care behind. Located 7 1/2 miles northwest of Two Harbors."

"WHERE YOU LEAVE DULL CARE BEHIND"
Located 7½ Miles Northeast of Two Harbors

Tom also served on the Minneapolis' Park Board. *The Pasadena Community Book,*** written later in 1943, credited him "with being largely responsible for the beautification and improvement of the Minneapolis parks which have a nation-wide reputation."

---

*Source: https://www.britannica.com/topic/*The-Woman-Citizen*.

***Pasadena Community Book: 1943.* William L. Blair Editor in Chief. Arthur H. Cawston Managing Editor and Publisher. Pasadena, California, 1943, p.453

1921-1924

Several important things happen before Edith's next letter. Betty's father, Charles Wilberforce Ames, dies in 1921 at age sixty-six. His wife, Mary Lesley Ames, continues to live at 501 Grand Avenue in St. Paul. She will turn seventy years old in 1924.

Betty marries Norris Dean Jackson in 1922. "The two grew up from babies as neighbors," wrote their daughter Leila. "My grandfather, John Norris Jackson, and grandmother, Alice Miller Dean Jackson – who was one of eight children – lived at 453 Grand Avenue east above the hill, now called Grand Hill."

John Jackson, back in about 1905, helped Charles Wilberforce and several other St. Paul businessmen found the St. Paul Academy which Norris, Betty's brothers and F. Scott Fitzgerald attended.

Even though Norris and Junior had been classmates at Princeton, they ran in different crowds. "My father was in the Ivy Club. Junior was not," Leila told me. "Daddy didn't like Junior."

I asked Leila to describe her father. ""He was about six feet tall, with a round face, and very dark black hair. He was a peacemaker, quiet spoken, thoughtful, just and fair. He had a magic way of getting people together. He had a great interest in other parts of the world and was always sending us children to the *Encyclopedia Britannica* – the 1911 Edition – to look things up. He played baseball, water polo and was a very good golfer. Unlike Junior, he didn't need to be celebrated.

"'Norris' was his grandmother's surname – Lucy Norris from New Hampshire. Edith called him 'Non' or 'Nonnie.' Oodles of others knew him as 'Uncle Non.'

"His grandfather Dean came from Pittsburgh – a world of river pilots, ship yards, power boats and steamboats. We know little about our Grandfather Jackson except that he was a grocer.

"After Princeton, Daddy started with the American Air Force and got stuck in Houston after training camp. He never went abroad. He went to work for his father's wholesale clothing company in St. Paul and remained there from 1919 to 1937."

The photo below of Betty and Norris was taken during their honeymoon in Cuba in January of 1923. Leila said, "They also traveled to the offshore islands and the Carolinas."

Getting back to Edith, she and Junior purchased or rented an apartment at 1330 North State Street, a few doors north of the fashionable Ambassador Hotel where, according to my Uncle Bud, "everything important happened. Our apartment took up the whole floor." Bud spent his early childhood running up and down the long central corridor.

My dad said his mother, Edith, traveled to stay with her mother, Alice, in Minneapolis for the births of all three sons. Bud was born on June 10, 1920. As mentioned, he was christened 'Knowlton Lyman Ames III.' His birth was announced in a Minneapolis newspaper.

Mrs. Knowlton Lyman Ames, Jr., and son, Knowlton Lyman Ames III.

My father, named Thomas Winter Ames – first called 'Tommy' – joined the family on July 16, 1922. He kept the photo above of himself, his mother and his brother Bud, which was taken in their Chicago apartment.

August 31, 1924
Chicago, Illinois

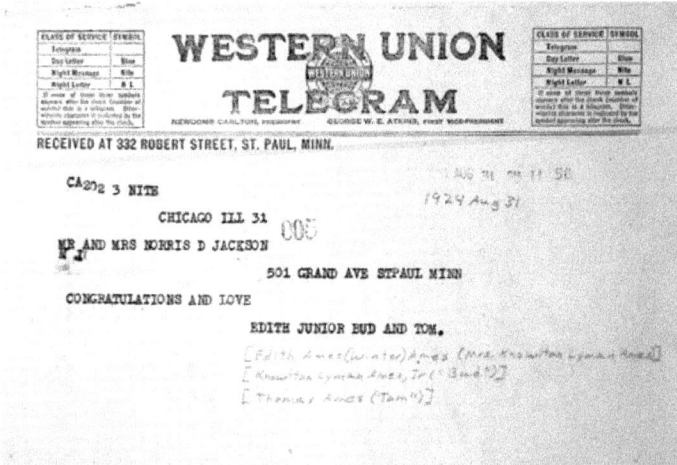

This telegram from Edith congratulates Betty and Norris on the birth of their first daughter, Leila Dean Jackson, in August of 1924. Catharine Ames Jackson, 'Kitty,' will arrive the next year in December of 1925. An English boy named Charles Morrison will join the girls during World War II. "We've always considered Charles part of the Ames family," said Leila. "Many English children were sent to safer places during the war. Twelve-year-old Charles' father was an Air Raid warden. When the war was over, Charles returned home on a destroyer. Eventually he became a doctor of anthropology. He died recently at age 87 in June, 2016."

WESTERN UNION TELEGRAM

Received at 332 Robert Street, St. Paul, Minn.
CA202 3 Nite, [Stamped] 1924 Aug 31 PM 11 58
Chicago Ill 31 005
Mr and Mrs Norris D Jackson
501 Grand Ave St Paul Minn
Congratulations and Love
Edith Junior Bud and Tom

1925

My Uncle Bob (Robert Dawes Ames) joined the male three-pack on November 15, 1925. I do not know how Edith and Junior chose the name Robert. 'Dawes' came from our ancestor William Dawes who rode with Paul Revere on the night of April 18, 1775, to help announce that General Howe's red-coats were marching toward Lexington and Concord.

1929

This note is from Betty to Edith. It appears to be a draft for a telegram sent from Boston to Chicago.

Mrs. K. L. Ames Jr.
1330 North State St.
Chicago.
Arriving Saturday
morning Burlington.
8.40 train time. Leaving
on Boston Wolverine.
Love to see you if
convenient
Betty
5026

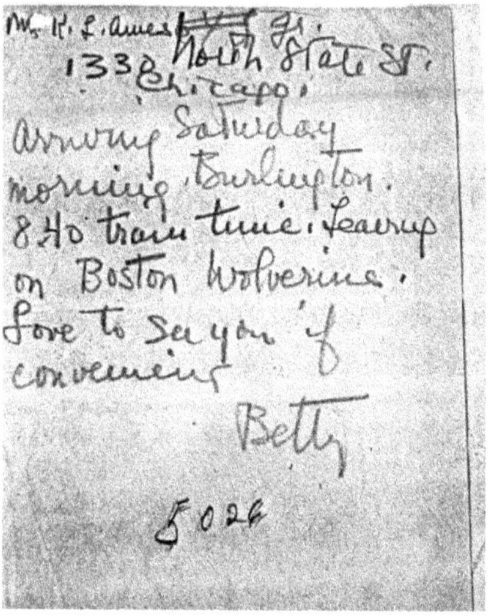

[To:] *Mrs. K. L. Ames Jr.*
1330 North State Street.
Chicago
Arriving Saturday morning Burlington
8.40 train time.
Leaving on Boston Wolverine.
Love to see you if convenient.
Betty

There is no further mention of Betty's visit.

Also during 1929, Betty's mother, Mary Lesley Ames, passed away. She
was seventy-five. Betty and Norris had already moved into 501 Grand to
help her during her last years. After Mary's death, Betty and her siblings
inherited the three-story home with its fourth-story attic.

Only Betty's family lived there, but her sister Margaret and family
lived next door. "Mummy was born and died in that house," said Kitty.
"Leila and I grew up there, too. We played in the huge room on the third
floor and put on events like play readings, which Grandpa Ames [Charles
Wilberforce] organized."

Norris took on the immense responsibility of the house's upkeep.
"Spring and fall he was on two-story ladders changing storm windows to
screens and vice versa," wrote Leila. "In later retirement years, he would
buy gallons of red paint or stain on sale to redo another section of the
narrow siding or upper shingles. Margaret and Cushing maintained the
large fenced side garden. There was a simple fountain she had begun with
her father when very young. Our mother loved plants and arranging
flowers in a special tile-floored, plant room in one corner of the house.
With Edith, she spent many happy hours in the screened side porch that
looked out over the garden, admiring the flowers and bushes while eating
lunch or chatting over tea."

Betty was more interested in what went on *in* the house. "Mummy
was a people person," Kitty said. "People were her hobby. 501 Grand
was like the family hotel. Exotic people came through our house all the
time. Social work was very important, too. Mummy started the St. Paul
chapter of the Junior League."

"Our mother was the neighborhood queen," added Leila, "the take-
charge person."

"But she didn't like to cook and sew," said Kitty. "In fact a seamstress
came to the house. I think our mother suffered from depression. She
seemed very fragile and slept a lot."

Bud and Tommy Ames in Nassau c.1930.

March 19, 1929
Chicago, Illinois

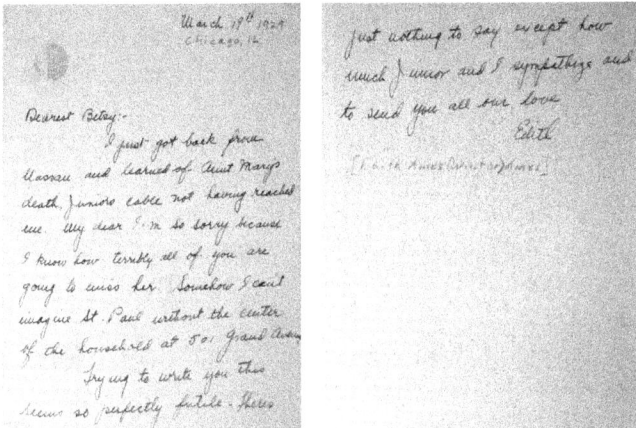

Like many wealthy residents of Chicago who wanted to escape the chilly winters, Junior purchased a vacation home in Nassau, the capital city of the Bahamas off the coast of Florida. According to his sister, Rosemary, who wrote extensively about the family, the house had the largest bar in the Bahamas. 'Juny,' as she called him, did a lot of entertaining there. Since the islands were British, there were no restrictions on alcohol consumption. Sometimes Edith and the boys joined Junior during the children's school holidays.

EWA

March 19th

Dearest Betsy:–

I just got back from Nassau and learned of Aunt Mary's death, Junior's cable not having reached me. My dear I'm so sorry because I know how terribly all of you are going to miss her. Somehow I can't imagine St. Paul without the center of the household at 501 Grand Avenue. Trying to write you this seems so perfectly futile – There's just nothing to say except how much Junior and I sympathize and to send you all our love.

Edith

⸺ ∞∞∞ ⸺

During this same year, Edith and Junior moved up North State Street – now referred to as State Parkway – from 1330 to 1530. They were among the first residents of the building, and again, their apartment took up an entire floor.

In 1989, columnist Michael Kilian* wrote an article for the *Chicago Tribune Magazine* that featured this apartment house. He titled the article "Inside Chicago Society: Who they are and how they live." Kilian wrote, "There are very specific addresses where the city's anointed abide, and it's very, very hard for the anointed to get in. These include ... 1530 N. State Pkw..."

Kilian also mentioned three exclusive social clubs to which Edith and Junior belonged. Uncle Bud told me, "Our family always were members of the Saddle and Cycle Club, until the time the family broke up. Your father Tommy, brother Bob and I spent countless days there, usually with our mother, enjoying its swimming pool and beach on Lake Michigan. It also had a par-three nine-hole golf course. Our mother was a member of the Casino Club for women and very active in it – often went there for cards, backgammon, etc. We were also members of the Racquet Club, which was a couple blocks from 1530 N. State, then only for men. You needed to sit next to Jesus to belong. Your father, brother Bob and I, as youngsters, were allowed to swim in their indoor pool on Saturdays, naked

───────────────

*Kilian, Michael. "Inside Chicago Society: Who they are and how they live," *Chicago Tribune Magazine*, November 5, 1989 Issue, Section 10, pp20

Reno

⊖⊗⊗⊖

Judging by the similar shirt collars, I am guessing that the formal portrait of Edith (left) taken in Chicago and the passport photo of Betty (right) were taken within the same decade. Betty will need a passport in 1937, when she takes her family to France, England and Scotland.

Meanwhile, a great deal happened between when Edith wrote the last letter in 1929 and the next letter from Reno, Nevada, in 1933. She is now in the process of getting a divorce.

Edith has made no reference to the stock market crash that devastated Junior's family and affected Edith's life extremely. Edith's father-in-law, Knowlton Lyman Ames, Sr., was overly leveraged in the market when it crashed. He was on a business trip in Europe when prices hit bottom. By the time he returned to the U.S., it was too late to salvage his empire.

Snake, as he was still known, owned a million dollar life insurance policy against his newspaper, *The Chicago Journal of Commerce*. On December 23, 1931, the day before the payment for the policy was due – and two days before Christmas – he told his chauffeur to stop at a drug store to purchase something for a headache. While the chauffeur was in the store making the purchase, Snake pulled a .38 caliber revolver out from under the seat of his car and shot himself in the head.

Betty must have seen the media accounts of the suicide. The news was plastered on the front page of every major newspaper in the country.

Ex-Football Player Shoots Self in Auto

Sends Servant for Medicine Before Action.

LAID TO ILLNESS

Famed Fullback at Princeton in 1890.

...ton L. Ames Sr., 63, ...der, financier, owner ...urnal of Commerce ...nbered the country "Snake" Ames of ...one of the greatest ...in football history, ... and killed himself last night.

Mr. Ames recently suffered a nervous breakdown and for a week had remained away from his office in the Booth Fisheries Company, 205 N. Michigan av. He was chairman of the board of the Booth company.

DINES WITH SISTER.

Last night his brother-in-law, Walter W. Ross, an attorney, met him in the loop and drove him to the Ross home at 1572 Ridge av.,

Knowlton L. Ames Sr.

FILE $1,398,690 CLAIM ON ESTATE OF K. L. AMES SR.

Bank Action Raises Total to $5,926,634.

Creditors of the late Knowlton L. Ames Sr., chairman of the board of the Booth Fisheries company, have filed claims totaling $5,926,634 against his estate in the Probate court. This aggregate was reached yesterday when the Central Republic Bank and Trust company filed a new claim of $1,398,690.

Mr. Ames, who killed himself last Dec. 31, left an estate of $50,000, according to his will, which was filed in the Probate court soon after his death. He also left an insurance trust of $1,100,000. The trust, however, has been held inviolate by Circuit Judge Thomas Taylor Jr., who gave his opinion recently that the trust funds could not be used to settle Mr. Ames' debts.

Claims by Bank.

The Central Republic bank's claim is composed of six divisions, as follows: $269,000 on Booth Fisheries notes which Mr. Ames guaranteed at the bank. $379,590 in notes of the Northwestern Fisheries company, which he also guaranteed; $112,850 in a note guaranteed for his son, John D. Ames; $50,000 in a note guaranteed for Charles H. Widman; Mr. Ames' personal note for $244,000, and $362,250 alleged to be owed for stock of the Booth Fisheries company which Mr. Ames contracted for but did not actually purchase from the bank.

The photocopied articles shown above were given to me by Snake's daughter, Rosemary, my great-aunt. You can find more information at http://en.wikipedia.org/wiki/Knowlton_Ames.

⊖⊗⊗⊖

Also missing from Edith's letters are accounts for why she is getting a divorce. According to her sons, Junior was a philanderer. According to her sister-in-law, Rosemary, 'Juny' drank too much. According to many accounts, the roaring twenties were fraught with dysfunctional behavior. Edith and Junior were from different cultures. Junior's father was a cut-throat businessman. Edith's father was a sedate, scholarly, church going, family man. Betty had predicted from the start that things would not work out.

1933
Reno, Nevada

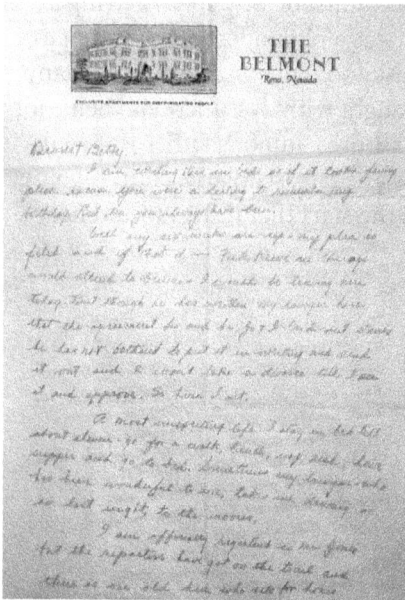

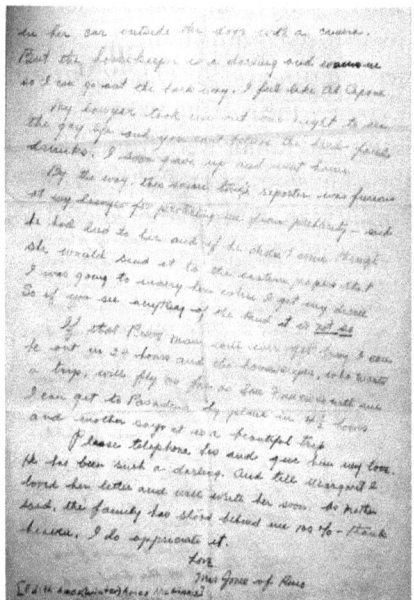

The scenario described in this letter could be a scene straight out of the hit play [and later movie] "The Women," written three years later in 1936 by Claire Booth Luce. If you have seen either the play or the movie, you will understand how this letter is a classic. Edith had taken a train to Nevada to obtain what my father always called, 'a Reno divorce.'

In 1933, divorces were difficult to obtain in most states, particularly in the Bible belt, which included Minnesota and Illinois. It was difficult to prove 'fault,' which in this case would have been adultery. The process was also socially messy. Proving that Junior was a verbal bully would have been equally socially awkward. However, if a person could prove he or she had been a resident of the state of Nevada for six or more weeks, he or she could legally obtain a 'no-fault divorce.'

Claire Booth Luce's play describes society-divorces like Edith's exactly – down to the detail of avoiding the photographers who came out from Chicago to take Edith's photo. This screen shot* from the movie shows the women biding their time on a ranch in Nevada while they wait for their six weeks to elapse.

The only major difference between the movie version and Edith's version is that the apartment house where Edith joined the like-minded "discriminating people" – as the letterhead on the Belmont Hotel stationery described them – looks a lot more comfortable than the cowboy ranch shown above.

---

*Image source for the screen shot from *The Women* movie: https://newyorktheater.files.wordpress.com/2014/12/the-women-clare-boothe-luce.jpg?w=630&h=499.

THE
BELMONT
Reno, Nevada

EXCLUSIVE APARTMENTS FOR DISCRIMINATING PEOPLE

Reno, Nevada
[1933]

Dearest Betsy:–

I am writing this in bed so if it looks funny please excuse. You were a darling to remember my birthday [December 7]. But then you always have been.

Well my six weeks are up – my plea is filed and if that d—— Fred Reeve in Chicago would attend to business I would be leaving here today. But though he has written my lawyer here that the agreement Les* and he, Jr & I laid out stands, he has not bothered to put it in writing and send it out and I won't take a divorce till I see it and approve. So here I sit.

A most unexerting[sic] life. I stay in bed till about eleven – go for a walk, brunch, nap, read, have supper and go to bed. Sometimes my lawyer — who has been wonderful to me, takes me driving or, as last night, to the movies.

I am officially registered as Mrs Jones but the reporters have got on the trail and there is one old hen who sits for hours in her car outside the door with a camera. But the housekeeper is a darling and warns me so I can go out the back way. I feel like Al Capone.

My lawyer took me out one night to see the gay life and you can't believe the hard-faced drunks! I soon gave up and went home.

By the way, this same tough reporter was furious at my lawyer for protecting me from publicity — said he had lied to her and if he didn't come through she would send it to the eastern papers that I was going to marry here where I got my decree. So if you see anything of the kind it is not so.

If that Reeve man will ever get busy I can be out in 24 hours and the housekeeper, who wants a trip, will fly as far as San Francisco with me. I can get to Pasadena by plane in 4 ½ hours and mother says it is a beautiful trip.

Please telephone Les and give him my love. He has been such a darling. And tell Margaret** I loved her letter and will write her soon. As mother said,

the family has stood behind me 100% — thank heaven. I do appreciate it.
Love
Mrs. Jones of Reno

---

*Betty's brother Les (Charles Lesley) became an attorney after graduating from Harvard and the St. Paul Law School [now part of Mitchell | Hamline School of Law].

**Just a reminder, 'Margaret' is Lesley and Betty's sister, married to Cushing F. Wright.

Tom and Alice Winter in their garden at 1230 Arroyo Boulevard.

Pasadena

December 25, 1933 [Christmas Day]
Pasadena, California

When Edith took the *Santa Fe* train to Reno, she left her three boys in
Chicago with a nurse. Bud was thirteen, Tom eleven, and Bob eight. After
the divorce went through, she traveled directly from Reno to Pasadena,
California, to live with her parents. Alice and Thomas Winter had moved
from Minneapolis to Pasadena seven years earlier in 1926. Thomas was
officially retired, due to poor health. But Alice had gone to work as the
Director of the Hayes Commission, the Hollywood organization that
rated and censored the movies.

After arriving in Pasadena, Edith sent for Tom and Bob. Bud told
me that he chose to stay with his father in Chicago, "a move I quickly
regretted when the old man packed me off to Shattuck Military Academy
so he could pursue wife number two." [Junior will marry three more times
and eventually retire with his fourth wife, Dorothy, on Harbour Island in
the Bahamas with thousands of chickens and a Capuchin monkey.]

Edith wrote this letter before Tom and Bob journeyed on the *Santa
Fe* to California by themselves, a trip they both would remember as being
a "lot of fun." She addressed it to Betty at 483 Grand Avenue in St. Paul
rather than 501 Grand. Leila explained this to me. "During the winter of
1933-1934, still Depression years, our household moved out of 501 and into
my grandparent's house at 483 Grand to save on heating and other costs."

Edith's handwriting on the envelope is a bit shaky. She addressed it
after a few eggnogs. I imagine it was very lonely for her after all the drama
she had been through. My father and uncles told me that their mother

suffered from alcoholism long before her divorce. Ironically, Prohibition ended on December 5, 1933, twenty days before Edith wrote this letter.

––––––––––––––

Mrs. Norris D. Jackson
483 Grand Avenue
St. Paul, Minnesota

1230 Dean Blvd. [Should be 1230 Arroyo Blvd]
Betsy darling:

I have been a pig not to have written you but honestly I was so on my tin ear what with things having to be corrected and hatred of Reno etc that I hadn't the courage. Now I am feeling fit again after dozens of egg-noggs, hours in bed, to say nothing of maternal* coddling and am my old self.

I got through on a private hearing on Monday and flew down here Tuesday and have done nothing but loaf and read ever since. I suppose you know Tom and Bob are to come out the first of February when they finish their school term. Then I will take a temporary furnished house near a good school and let them finish out the year. When Bud comes when he finishes school I hope to find a cottage somewhere on the sea for the summer and then come back and get a permanent abode and have my furniture sent out.

The weather is divine. I can ride in an open car without a coat and I got a sunburn this morning sitting in the patio. I went to a reception yesterday with the parents where a lot of small children sang carols and we all ate a lot and it was quite fun. Now I shall have to concentrate on remembering the names and faces of the people I meet, and you know how bad I am at that.

The nurse writes me that the children are well and planning a splendid Christmas and as she is a better mother to them than I am, I am sure they will be all right.

I had the darlingest colored maid in Reno. She was young but she loved me like a mother and one day she got Tom Ryan, my lawyer, to take me for an all day drive and when I got back she had arranged a surprise party of seven of the nicest people I had met and gave us a huge dinner of fruit cup, soup, turkey, three vegetables, mashed potatoes, and for desert ice cream made to look exactly like a birthday cake with 16 candles and "Happy Birthday Edith" in pink icing. And had done it all herself, she is a marvelous cook. So you see I wasn't too fo[r]lorn. Do call Les and give him my love and say I will write soon. And my best to you darling.

Edith

Thursday, 1933
Pasadena

According to Uncle Bud, his grandparents Winter moved out of the main house of 1230 North Arroyo Boulevard in Pasadena and into their guest cottage to make room for their daughter and her sons. Bud lived with them during school holidays while attending Stanford. He remembered the paving stones in the grass leading from the house to the guest house. Betty went to visit Edith in Pasadena and took these photos. On the back of the first photo she wrote a note that the Winters had completed building the home in 1928.

Decades later, I lived a few blocks north of 1230 at 1715 La Cresta. My house also perched on the edge of the dry river canyon known as the Arroyo Seco [aka Arroyo Seco Park].

Arroyo Boulevard runs along the east edge of the canyon that cuts north to south through otherwise flat Pasadena. The Rose Bowl stadium was built in the middle of the park four years before the Winters moved there, in 1922. The view from the front lawn of 1230 overlooks the stadium and the spacious canyon. To the north rise the majestic foothills of the Sierra Madres. As I looked at that same view from the terrace of my house at 1715 La Cresta, I felt as if the space around me was endless, even though I was in the middle of a city. It was very peaceful.

The streets on both sides of the canyon are lit at night with round glass bulbs. According to Uncle Bud's version of the family lore, one warm Pasadena evening, as Alice and Thomas stood on their lawn looking out over the canyon, Thomas likened the lights to strings of glowing pearls. "I wish I could afford to give you the real thing," he said to his wife.

1230 No Arroyo Blvd
Thursday

Dear Betsy:

At last the decks seem to be cleared for action – I am free, white and twenty one and Feb 2nd I will be in my own house – with a guest room which I hope you will occupy. Do come out if you can. You will find me a changed woman – almost sane and normal.

Tom and Bob are due here on the 4th and start school on the fifth. I get into my house on the 2nd and will start life as a California matron.

This time with father and mother has been a grand breathing spell and has put me back on my feet. But I am anxious to be on my own once more. I have been going to teas which all the old ladies here take very seriously and you wear what practically amounts to an evening dress and leave cards and see the same people. I am actually beginning to distinguish them (the people) at least the ones with lots of lace and long chains of beads are women and the ones with mustaches and bad teeth used to be men.

Father seems even better than he was 19 months ago, but I am afraid mother is doing too much. But she admits herself that if she gives up her job she will feel definitely on the shelf, and as no one can stop what is the matter with her prehaps[sic] *she is better off going on.* [Alice had something wrong with her head that made it swell – probably a brain tumor.] *But of course she worries me.*

And how are all the Jacksons, big and little? Do come out if you can and we will read, sew, go to movies and lead the quiet life I see stretching before me. If you need a rest, and Les says you do, it will do you good, and it would be grand for me.

Love, Edith

––––––––––––––

My father told me that his mother rented a small cottage on California Terrace about a half mile south of where her parents lived, but still on the east side of Pasadena, and still near the Arroyo Seco.

My grandmother's description of starting out life as a divorced woman in Pasadena reminds me of when I was in the same position at about the same age in 1983. I received similar reactions from other Pasadena society matrons. Some things do not change.

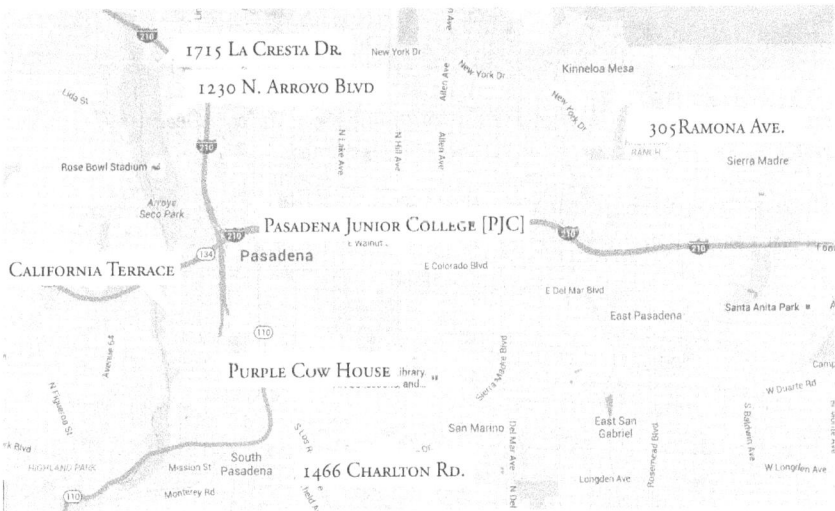

This GoogleMap shows the location of California Terrace and some of the other places Edith will talk about and/or visit in Pasadena.

———∽∾∿———

Edith writes her next letter from a beach house. Tom and Alice built one of the first vacation homes in San Malo at the southern edge of Oceanside. It sits 92 miles south of Pasadena and 53 miles north of San Diego. As he had done with Minneapolis' park system, Tom helped organize the building of the Normandy-style gated community. He was familiar with Normandy style architecture because, as already mentioned, he attended college in San Malo, Normandy, France, before migrating to Canada. He returned to Normandy during World War I.

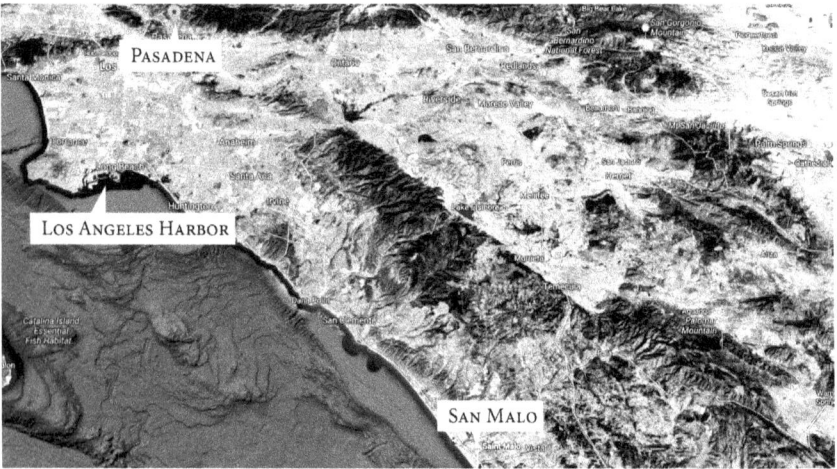

GoogleMaps3D showing the location of San Malo in Oceanside in relation to Pasadena.

These photos, taken some time before June of 1934, were among my father's family documents.

Epatant.

*La Plage de S Malo.
Oceanside. C*

*Alice and Tom Winter at their beach house in
San Malo, Oceanside, California*

June 22, 1934

Two months before writing the next letter, on June 22, 1934, Edith's father, Thomas Gerald Winter, passed away. He was seventy-one – two years older than his wife, Alice. His ashes were buried in the Lakewood Cemetery in Minneapolis alongside Alice's father (Charles Gordon Ames), mother (Fanny Baker Ames), Fanny's mother (Julia Ann Canfield Baker), and his son, Gilbert. I took the above photo of the grave-site in 2005.

Gilbert is the first name engraved at the top of the cross. I suspect the elaborate Celtic cross – a style adopted by the Presbyterians in Scotland – Thomas had a lot of Scottish ancestry – was created right after Gilbert's premature death.

Though Edith does not mention it, she and Alice flew to Minneapolis to attend her father's funeral and burial. Betty and Norris Jackson attended, too. Therefore, the cousins saw each other a few months before Edith wrote this from the beach house.

August 28, 1934
Probably **San Malo, Oceanside, California**

Forgive the goofy paper. They printed it wrong and I have to use it up.
[Arrow to the monogram printed backwards.]

From Tom:
Dear Aunt Betty & Uncle Nony:
Thank you for the book of "The Swallows & Amazons" I sure am tan. Brownie our dog ran away. We are only going to stay at the beach for three more days. [I] had a boy down here for a few days.
Love Tom

Bob wrote:
I thank you for the "Book Cowboy Tom"
Love Bob.

Starting on the second page, Edith wrote:
Dear Bet and Non:-
Thanks Non; for your letter. It was dear of you to think of it. And the children loved their books.
You will be glad to know that I have been completely on the wagon for the last six weeks and expect to remain so.
It has been a quiet summer. Mother has been down for long week ends so I haven't tried having any company – except last week end when I had a nice couple – an odd man, and a little boy. The walls were practically

bulging.

We move to town Friday and will be at mother's over the week-end when I hope to be established in a little house. Tom is going to the Midland Ranch school [in Los Olivos] *this winter and Bob to the Ojai Valley* [School], *so I may sub-let the house and go about a bit. I don't have any definite plans yet.*

The boys have had a perfect summer and are a deep mahogany color. They swim most of the time and we have had lots of weinie[sic] *roasts on the beach and there are lots of children for them to play with.*

I may turn up in St. Paul for a few days – who can tell. Tell Les I am writing him a long delayed letter soon.

Love to both, Edith

My dad told me that the Midland School was for troublesome boys. Secluded in a rustic environment, the students took on everyday chores not required by most boarding schools. He was not at all happy there and after one year, his mother pulled him out and sent him to Pasadena public schools where he thrived.

September 23, 1936 [photo from the 1950s]
Pasadena, California

Edith's surviving letters do not mention that she met and married Paul McGinnis three years after her divorce. Unitarian minister H.W.G. Soares officiated their wedding in Pasadena on September 23, 1936.

I found the marriage certificate among my father's family papers. It states that Paul formerly resided at 951 S. Lucerne Blvd. in nearby Los Angeles. He was the son of Cilliam T. McGinnis of Minnesota and Carrie McCord of Wisconsin. At thirty-nine years old (one year younger than Edith), he had not been previously married. Paul listed his occupation as "Power House Operator at a Power Generator." According to my Uncle Bob, the power generator in Saugus, 33.9 miles northwest of Pasadena near the Angeles National Forest, generated power for Los Angeles from water rushing from the Colorado River.

Paul was also a writer. We will hear more about that later. The flyleaf of the book he will write stated that he was a "reporter, editor, and magazine writer" who "grew up in Colorado but came East to attend Columbia University. After graduating from Columbia School of Journalism, he joined the staff of the *New York Daily News* as a reporter and later moved to the *New York Evening Journal* in an editorial capacity. It was during the war, while he aided in testing Lockheed flight equipment that some of his most exciting magazine writing was done." The flyleaf also stated that his wife, Edith, was "also an author."

Paul was an inventor as well. Among my father's papers on him were copies of a patented drawing of an oil can. Like other oil cans, it looks like the hat that the Tin Man wore in the movie *The Wizard of Oz*. What made Paul's oil can special was that it squirted while being held upside down. It could be used when oiling something in a tight place, such as from under a car.

I loved my pipe-smoking 'Grandpa Paul.' I never met my real grandfather, Junior, because he and my dad became estranged before I was born. [I wrote all about that in my book about my father titled *The Man in the Purple Cow House*.] Everyone liked Paul except my father, who, according to Uncle Bud, "found him competition for time with our mother."

My memories of Paul are that he loved playing golf and usually wore a golf shirt. He showed me how to do card tricks and taught me how to double shuffle the cards in one move. He was shorter than my grandmother. In photos of them together, she stoops.

August, 1937

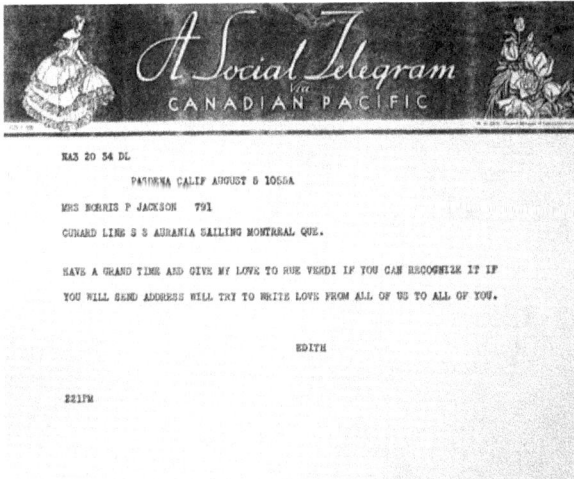

Betty is taking her husband and two daughters to France to show them where she lived and worked during World War I. Their boat, the *Aurania*, sails from Montreal, Canada. "My mother sold $2000 worth of General Motors stock to pay for that trip," said Leila. "Her attitude was, 'If you have something you want to do, then do it.' But later, she had to borrow money to pay for our furnace at 501 to be repaired."

———————

A SOCIAL TELEGRAM VIA
CANADIAN PACIFIC

NA3 30 34 DL
                    Pasadena Calif August 5 1055A [10:55 AM]
Mrs Norris P Jackson T91
Cunard Line S S Aurania Sailing Montreal Que. [Quebec]
Have a grand time and give my love to rue Verdi if you can recognize it. If you will send address will try to write. Love from all of us to all of you.
                    Edith

January 14th, 1938

Betty, Norris, Leila and Kitty returned from the trip mentioned in the above telegraph in October of 1937. Edith wrote this letter three months later. By now, her mother, Alice, has given Edith and Paul her home at 1230 North Arroyo and moved to a smaller house around the corner at 1235 Solita Road.

———————

MRS. PAUL McGINNIS • 1230 NO ARROYO BLVD.
PASADENA • CALIFORNIA

January 14th

Dear Betsy:-

Such lovely handkerchiefs. They look and smell Paris, and I adore them.

I sent you a wire to the boat where you sailed, and hoped to hear whether you thought Rue Verdi attractive in its new guise, but I know how impossible it is to write when you are travelling and what a family you have to write to anyway.

Mother, Paul, and I have just come back from five days at 29 Palms [Palm Springs], *lost off in the desert 50 miles from anything. It was doctors orders for mother but she wouldn't go till I practically hauled her off. What we did, you can see, is Paul's drawing of our cottage – and we all feel much better for it. I dashed for the garden when we got home last night and found first bloom on my larkspur and sweet-peas — Rain coming today so I got a*

*couple of bags of manure, this being the day the gardener comes, and they
are all over the front and patio lawns.*

You would be much amused at how crazy I am about the garden.

*Tom comes in from school tomorrow to get a new suit to wear to a
dance at the Westridge girls school* [in Pasadena] *that night. He went to a
dinner dance with Ed Foley's daughter Margaret during vacation and I ran
into Dorothy Thompson when I took him over there. I see Lil Yeates off and
on and she is exactly the same. Do write.*

Love, Edith

⸙

We have another big jump in time. Europe is at war again. "From the fall
of 1939," said Leila, "to the end of the war, our attic at 501 Grand served
as a clothing factory — the 'Betty Ames Jackson branch of the British
war relief.' My mother's sister Margaret, and husband Cushing, who lived
next door, were the shipping department."

Edith makes no mention of war relief efforts in Pasadena. Her son
Bud is a student at Stanford University, thanks to the good will of his
grandmother, Alice. Tom is a student at Pasadena Junior College, which
was on the same campus as the high school – commonly referred to as
'PJC.' Bob attends 'South Pass High,' a.k.a. South Pasadena high school,
which, in those days, included students from South Pasadena as well as
the more POSH suburb of San Marino.

December 24, 1939
Pasadena

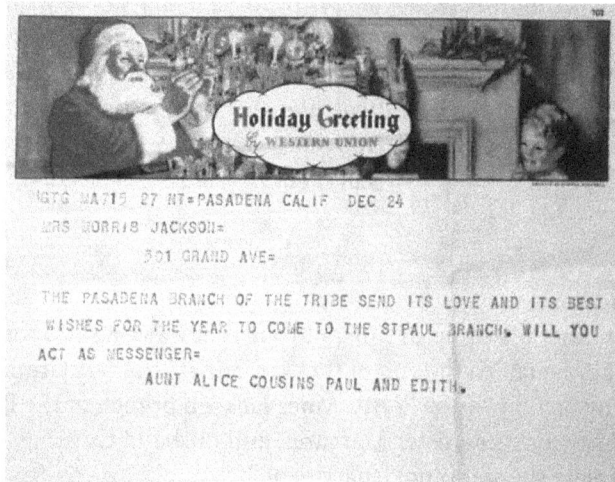

HOLIDAY GREETING
WESTERN UNION

GTG MA 715 27 NT= PASADENA CALIF DEC 24
Mrs. Norris Jackson
    501 Grand Ave
The Pasadena branch of the tribe send its love and its best wishes for the year to come to the St. Paul branch. Will you act as messenger.
        Aunt Alice, cousins, Paul and Edith.

April 5, 1944
Pasadena

In none of these surviving letters does Edith mention the death of her mother in Pasadena on April 4, 1944. Betty saved this article that was published the next day, probably in the *Pasadena Star News*.

Mrs. Thomas G. Winter, Noted Clubwoman, Dies

Mrs. Thomas G. Winter, 78, one of the nation's outstanding clubwomen and for many years director of the department of studio and public service of the Motion Picture Producers and Distributors of America, Inc., died at her home, 1235 Solita Road, Pasadena, yesterday after a long illness. She was the widow of Thomas Gerald Winter, wealthy grain broker, and from 1929 worked with the Will Hays office.

Federation President: A distinguished author* and lecturer, Mrs.

Winter was president of the General Federation of Women's Clubs from 1920 to 1924, and both before and after served as chairman of the federation's literature and international relations committees.

During World War I she was head of Minnesota Women's Council of Defense and subsequently was appointed to the advisory committee of the Conference on the Limitation of Armaments by President Harding.

Wellesley Graduate: A native of Albany, N.Y. Mrs. Winter was graduated from Wellesley College with both bachelor's and master's degrees. In 1938 she was awarded the honorary degree of doctor of human letters by the University of Southern California.

With her at the time of her passing were her daughter and son-in-law, Mr. and Mrs. Paul McGinnis. She also leaves three grandsons, K.L. [Knowlton Lyman], Thomas W. and Robert D. Ames, all in the United States Army.

Her funeral will be conducted at 2 p.m. Saturday at the McGinnis residence, 1230 N. Arroyo Blvd., Pasadena. The body will be sent to Minneapolis for internment."

----

*Books written by Alice Vivian Ames Winter:

1905: Winter, Alice. with drawings by R. M. Crosby. *The Prize to the Hardy*, The Bobbs-Merrill Company Publishers, Indianapolis

1906: Winter, Alice Ames. with illustrations by Harrison Fisher. *Jewel Weed*, The Bobbs-Merrill Company Publishers, Indianapolis

1925: Winter, Alice Ames. President of the General Federation of Women's Clubs, 1920-1924. *The Business of Being a Club Woman*, The Century Co, New York & London

1927: Winter, Alice Ames. *The Heritage of Women*, Minton, Balch & Company, New York.

As the news clipping noted, Edith's three boys had gone off to participate in World War II. Bud was the first of the brothers to join the service. He entered as an officer because he had attended Shattuck Military School. During most of the war, he served as the editor of the Army's *YANK* magazine, stationed first in Alexandria, Egypt, then in Saipan in the Pacific.

According to the news article below, the youngest brother, Bob, "was a staff sergeant with the 15th Air Force and flew 35 missions over Germany as aerial gunner, earning six battle stars, the Air Medal and three clusters."

My dad, Tom, the middle brother, stayed stateside and worked for the Army's Psychological Testing Department, mainly at Sheppard's Field, an air base in Texas.

Some time after the memorial reception for Alice on North Arroyo, Edith and Paul sold that home and purchased another one at 1466 Charlton Road in San Marino just south of Pasadena. That is where my Uncle Bud remembered staying with them for a few days when he was traveling through Pasadena on his way from Egypt to Saipan.

On November 23, 1945, three months after V-Day Europe, Edith's youngest son, Bob, married his high school sweetheart, Kathryn "Kay" Ann Wallace. They had met when they were fifteen years old attending PJC [Pasadena Junior College].

Mr. and Mrs. R. D. Ames To Reside in North; Now in Santa Barbara

By RUTH BILLHEIMER, Society Editor

MASSES of white chrysanthemums at the church and reception made lovely settings for nuptials uniting Miss Kathryn Ann Wallace and Robert Dawes Ames and for their attendant festivities Friday evening. Two hundred and fifty guests were invited by the bride's parents, Mr. and Mrs. Leonard Lewis of East Foothill Boulevard, Altadena, to 8 o'clock rites in St. Mark's Episcopal Church. A reception followed at the home of the bridegroom's parents, Mr. and Mrs. Paul McGinnis of Charlton Road, San Marino.

Candles twinkled at the altar as the bridal party entered the church to measures of the Wedding March from "Lohengrin." Flowers affixed to alternate pew ends bordered the aisle as Mr. Wallace escorted his daughter to the waiting bridegroom. Preceding them were the bride's three attendants, all in pink.

The attendants wore jersey gowns, draped in modern fashion, necklines low and squared, short sleeves softly draped. Each of the three wore matching mitts and in her hair was a coronet of rose buds to match her bouquet.

Gown Was Mother's

Miss Rosalind Stapleton, who was maid of honor, carried American Beauty roses, to distinguish her from the bridesmaids, Miss Barbara Pardridge of Pasadena and Mrs. William Wheeler Parks (Marjorie Hayes) of Hermosa, who carried pale pink buds.

The bride followed them in her lovely white satin gown, which had been worn by her mother 25 years ago. The gown was restyled according to present modes, its sweetheart neckline set off by encrustation of pearls cross the shoulders in a deep yoke effect. The skirt ended in a train and veil, held by a tiara of tiny pearls, was of three-quarters length. To complete the picture, the bride carried a bouquet of bouvardia centered with a large white orchid, which later she wore on her traveling suit.

Thomas Ames attended his brother as best man and the ushers were Harold Hanson, Robert Westcott, Warren Rogers, Jerald Scott and Stephen Whittlesy.

Mrs. Wallace wore a stunning

AMES-WALLACE: See Page 10

MRS. ROBERT DAWES AMES
(Kathryn Ann Wallace)

Ames-Wallace

(Continued)

black and white gown. Its white crepe top was studded with rhinestones and the skirt made of draped black velvet. Her headdress matched the bodice and she wore a corsage of gardenias.

Mrs. McGinnis' costume was of pale blue, embellished with crystal beading, and in her hair she wore a coronet of pale blue ostrich tips. Her flowers also were gardenias.

Dr. Stephen Cutter Clark, rector of St. Mark's, performed the ceremony and Marcia Hannah, organist, provided the wedding music.

The bride cut the wedding cake in a bay window of the dining room where it was arranged with white flowers upon a small round table. Later when she and Mr. Ames left for their wedding trip, she had changed to a brown suit whose

shoulders and sleeves were capped with beaver and she wore a little matching half-hat, beaver trimmed.

Mr. Ames has taken his bride to Santa Barbara where they will spend part of their honeymoon at Hotel El Encanto. They will go on to Palo Alto, where they plan to reside after Jan. 1, but will be South again for the Christmas holidays.

Mrs. Ames is a graduate of Pasadena Junior College where she belonged to The Club and was Tab editor for two and a half years. Her husband, recently discharged from the Army Air Force, is also an alumnus of P. J. C. and attended California Preparatory School.

Mr. Ames was a staff sergeant with the 15th Air Force and flew 33 missions over Germany as aerial gunner, earning six battle stars, the Air Medal and three clusters. He is a grandson of the late Mrs. Thomas G. Winter.

Tom and Bud were home from the Army in time to attend the wedding along with 250 other guests. Tom served as Bob's best man. Kay's father led her down the aisle to the same wedding march to which Edith's father had led her down the aisle twenty-six years earlier in 1919, Wagner's 'Lohengrin.' Edith and Paul hosted the reception at their home on Charlton Road in San Marino.

THE NEW YORK TIMES, MONDAY, MARCH 10, 1947.

BRIDES-TO-BE

MISS JAYNE SKIRM ENGAGED TO MARRY

Bradford Alumna Will Be Wed to Knowlton L, Ames 3d, a Former Official of Yank

Mr. and Mrs. William H. Skirm 3d of 8 East Eighty-third Street have announced the engagement of their daughter, Jayne Rubicam, to Knowlton L. Ames 3d, son of Mrs. Paul McGinnis of Pasadena, Calif., and Knowlton L. Ames. Jr.

The prospective bride was graduated from the George School in Bucks County, Pa., and, class of '44, from Bradford Junior College. She is with the editorial department of McCalls Magazine. Her father is an executive of Young & Rubicam, Inc., the advertising firm here.

Mr. Ames, an alumnus of Stanford University, was honorably discharged recently as a major after serving as publications officer and acting business manager of Yank, the Army weekly magazine. His father is a former publisher of The Evening Post in Chicago, and his uncle, John D. Ames, is publisher of The Chicago Journal of Commerce.

Miss Jayne Rubicam Skirm
David Berns

As you can see, Edith's oldest son, Bud (Knowlton Lyman Ames III), is about to get married on June 21, 1947, to Jayne Rubicam Skirm of New York. Many years later – when Uncle Bud was in his eighties – he told me with a great deal of bitterness that my father did not attend the ceremony. Bud held that grudge for a long time. Bud and Jayne's oldest child, Jeff, sent me this clipping from the *New York Times. The Chicago Sunday Tribune* will announce the marriage on June 22.

June 8, 1947
San Marino, California

1466 CHARLTON ROAD
SAN MARINO, CALIFORNIA

June 8 '47

Dearest Betsy:–

Somehow, via the family grapevine, you may have heard that Paul and I are going east for Bud's wedding. We can't afford it but I simply couldn't bear not to go. We fly to Chicago on Wednesday, drive to N.Y. with Bud and stay there, at the Hotel Stanhope, 5th Ave & 81st till the 22nd – spend a night with Virginia Viall MacLeod in Saunderstown and then to Boston to see Alice, Ted & Aunt Edith. What worries me is that I may miss your children if they decide to come to California. What are their plans? Tom will be here and of course they are welcome to the house but I do so want to know them.

We went to an enormous (325) party at Annandale [still a private golf club in the Pasadena foothills] *last night and I ran into Kitty MacCahill*

Lane [somehow related to Betty's ex-fiancé Ted Lane]– *funny after all these years, and sat next to a man who was brought up in Yarmouth* [where Edith and Raymond Crosby lived] *and whose wife went to school with Katherine Crothers* [sister of Betty's brother-in-law Bronson Crothers.*]

*Doesn't anyone in the family like "Lost Eden?"*** We haven't had any comment.*

Love,
Edith

---

*Bronson Crothers went to Harvard with Betty's brother Lesley Ames. Eventually he became a well renowned neurologist for children. Kitty Wise recently told me that a book I had in my library, that had been left to me by my father, was written by Bronson and Katherine's father, Samuel McChord Crothers (1857-1927), a respected Unitarian minister. He was a generation younger than Charles Gordon Ames. *The Dame School of Experience* is signed by Samuel Crothers' to "Alice Ames Winter, 1920." A torn piece of newspaper still serves as a bookmark on page 37. I haven't read the book yet.

**Lost Eden* was the book Paul wrote. I found two copies for sale on the Internet – one on E-Bay for $50 and another on ReadInk.com for $60. I bargained for the E-Bay version and bought it for $20.

The novel is about Captain Cook's final voyage to the South Seas told from the point of view of the botanical illustrator on the expedition. "No wonder Paul and my grandmother wanted to live in Hawaii," I thought after reading it. I was amazed Paul knew so much about Captain Cook and his times. I wish I had read the book while Paul was still alive so I could ask him about it. Leila remembered reading *Lost Eden* "as a young girl from the bookshelf of 501 Grand." Therefore we know Betty had a copy.

Before **June 22, 1947**
New York City

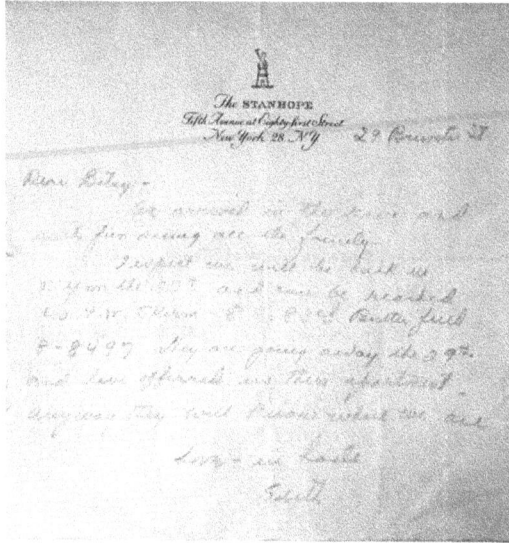

THE STANHOPE
FIFTH AVENUE AT EIGHTY-FIRST STREET
NEW YORK 28, NY

29 Brewster Street

Dear Betsy:–
We arrived in the rain and such fun seeing all the family.
I expect we will be back in N.Y. on the 27th and can be reached c/o
H.W. Skirm – 8 E. 83rd Butterfield 8-8497. They are going away the 29th
and have offered us their apartment – anyway they will know where we are.
Love – in haste

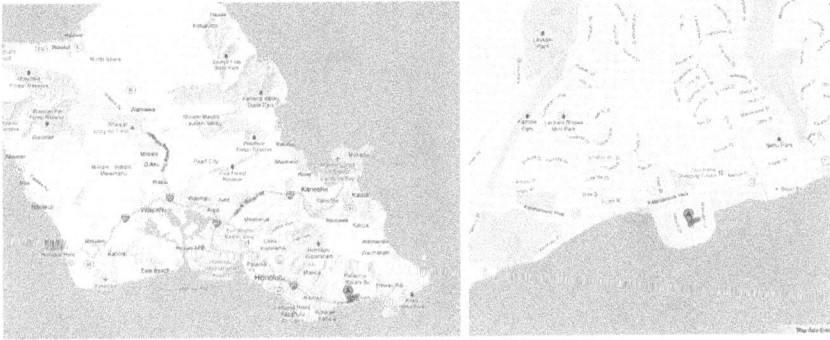

28 Niuhi Street, Honolulu, Oahu, Hawaii. (GoogleMaps).

Honolulu

—⊶∞⊷—

It is three years later. Edith and Paul moved to a suburb of Honolulu, Hawaii, some time before May of 1946 when Leila remembers her mother suggesting that the St. Paul family go to Hawaii to visit them.

Bud and Jane are living in Chicago. Bob and Kay have moved to Turlock, California. My father has graduated from the University of California Berkeley with an engineering degree and set up a landscaping business in Pasadena. Two months earlier, on July 11, 1950, he married my mother, Eileen Mary Hopkins, known as 'Betty May.' Edith and Paul did not fly to California for the wedding, which was held at my great-grandmother Mary Hopkins' house in Santa Barbara, nor did they attend the wedding reception held in Pasadena. Instead, they sent my father and his bride, for a wedding present, tickets for an ocean liner to take them to Hawaii for their honeymoon. Tom and Betty May stayed with Edith and Paul at their new house. My mother, who was a virgin when she married, thought that spending one's honeymoon under the same roof as her new in-laws was a bit odd, but told me she had a good time.

Santa Barbara Garden Wedding
Joins Eileen Hopkins, Thomas Ames

With several Pasadenans numbered in the intimate gathering attendant upon rites yesterday afternoon, two popular young people from this city were married in Santa Barbara. They are Miss Eileen Mary Hopkins, daughter of Pryns Hopkins, former Pasadenan who now resides on Garden Street, Santa Barbara and Thomas Winter Ames, son of Mrs. Paul McGinnis of Honolulu, formerly of San Marino. He is a grandson of the late Mrs. Thomas G. Winter of Pasadena.

The bride and bridegroom have left for a honeymoon in Honolulu and will visit Mr. and Mrs. McGinnis. They will make their home temporarily at 55 Arlington Drive, on their return, Aug. 1 and plan to build in Pasadena.

Four o'clock was the hour appointed for the ceremony, performed by Dr. Eugene Sill, Congregational clergyman, in the gardens of the bride's grandmother, Mrs. Charles Harris Hopkins. Miss Marcia Kober of Pasadena was maid of honor and the bride's sister, Miss Jennifer Hopkins of Santa Barbara, was bridesmaid.

Robert Dawes Ames of Turlock served his brother as best man. Ushers were the bride's brother, David Hopkins of Santa Barbara, Theodore Newton and Allen Coon of Pasadena.

The bridal party assembled before an improvised altar of greenery in the patio of Mrs. Hopkins' lovely oak - shaded gardens. A white motif was carried out with flowering white potted plants. The bride selected an ankle-length frock of champagne organdy embroidered in white and inset with bands of white Val lace. A tiny cap of champagne velvet studded with brilliants held a shoulder length illusion veil and she wore long, sheer gloves. Her suede slippers matched her dress and she carried a bouquet of white orchids with golden throats.

Miss Kober's dress was navy voile with white accents. With it she wore white gloves and a wide, navy horsehair hat with velvet crown and trimming. Miss Hopkins wore white dotted Swiss with Val lace trim and a crown of daisies. Each attendant carried an armful of the same flowers.

A green-and-white motif was employed also for the garden reception at which the triple-tiered wedding cake was cut. Among the guests participating were Messrs. and Mmes. Edgar Irving Kober of San Marino, Frederick R. Huggins

—Wanek-King Photo.

MRS. THOMAS WINTER AMES

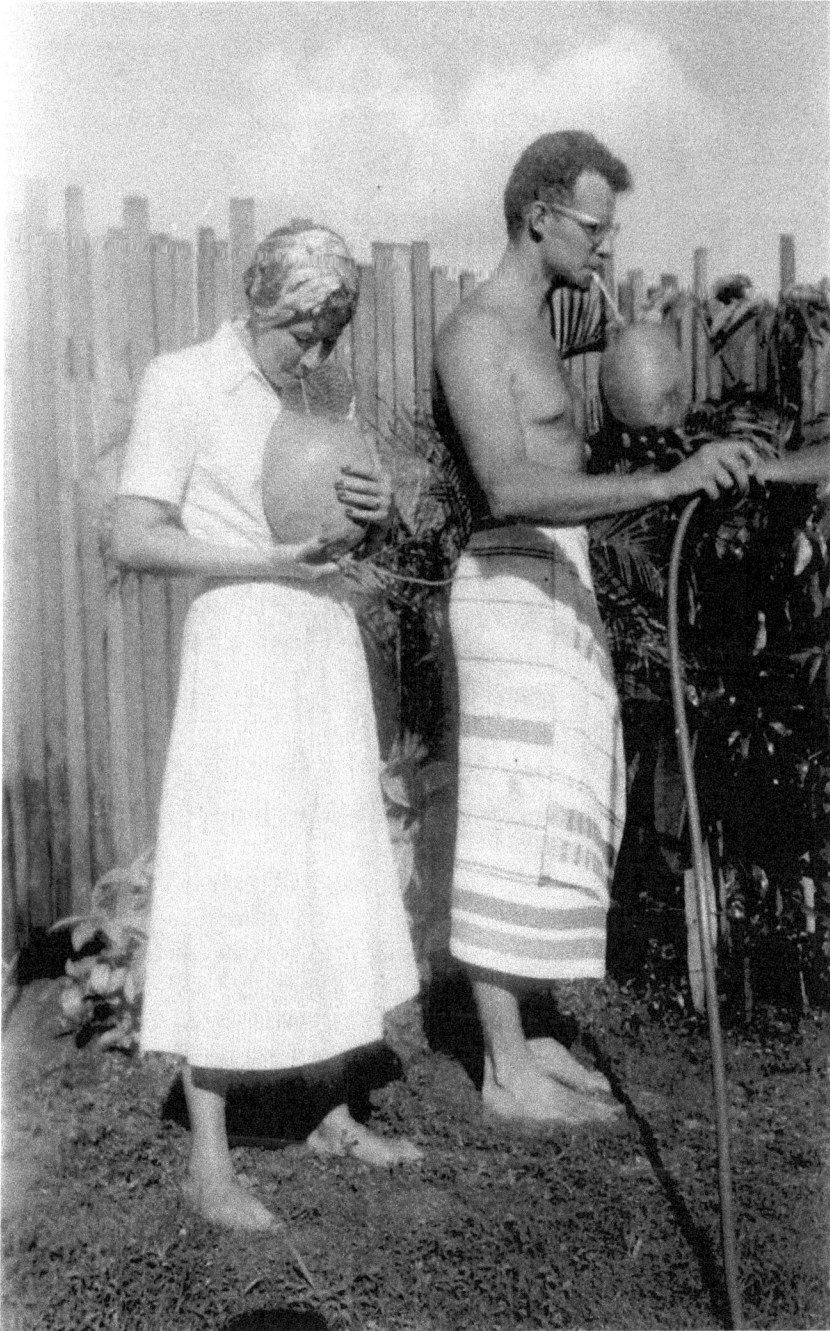

Betty May and Tom Ames on their honeymoon in Hawaii.

Edith and Paul hired architect Vladimir Ossipoff to design their house for them. Uncle Bud saved the *Sunset Magazine* article from September 1952. My dad saved the December 19, 1953 issue of Honolulu's *Star Bulletin*. Written by the same person, they give us some insight into Edith and Paul's lifestyle.

A generous house, yet frugal with space

As a writer, Paul McGinnis of Honolulu expected his home to give him efficient working conditions and many unconfined, interesting backgrounds for loafing. Mrs. McGinnis' demands for efficiency and individual use were just as exacting. ... the owners and architect Vladimir Ossipoff followed two planning principles: They borrowed space from a well-protected, private garden; they forced rooms to perform double duty in use. Note the 24 by 15-foot living room. With glass on both entry and lanai side, the room is the protected center of a tropical garden.

Visually the green walls of the garden become the living room walls, while the lanai doubles the roof-protected space. The dining section of the living room, doubling as a game room, has its own close garden association. [A detail photograph shows how the dining table closes up to become a card table.] The kitchen, with extra wide counters serves well as a sewing room. When work schedules permit, study-office can be converted into a guest room.

September 10, 1950
Honolulu, Hawaii

EWMG
[EDITH WINTER MCGINNIS]

28 Niuhi St. Honolulu
Sept 10

Dearest Betsy:–
The millennium has arrived a letter from you even though it took a Korean war to produce it. I have written Jim Turner [son of Betty's sister, Catharine Turner] *and hope he will get in touch with us, so we can get to know him, and perhaps provide him with a little amusement. As to this cemetery business* [Lakewood Cemetery in Minneapolis where her mother was buried] *— I have heard nothing from them. Aren't they the limit! Sometime will you ask Lesley if he has any ownership deed to the cemetery lot. There is one space left - more if cremated, and I think Aunt E. should have it, though it's a bit delicate to tell her so. As I shall probably*

die here I might as well be planted under the frangipani trees. I would prefer being scattered on the waves but they do that only for the beach boys.

We were so disappointed you and Nonnie didn't get here. We heard rumors you might come and kept on hoping. Tom & Betty May (how they got that name out of Eileen Mary) were here twelve days of violent gayety on their honeymoon.

She is grand. Not pretty but with beautiful instinctive manners and lots of charm and just right for Tom. For a wedding present her family gave them enough money to put up a building next to Tom's greenery – office space below and a big room plus kitchen, bath + sun deck for them to live in above. The office space to rent for income. Weren't they lucky.

Bob and Kay are living in Turlock, Calif. which is ghastly in summer. After one year as advertising salesman he has been made advertising manager of the Turlock Journal. As he is only 24 we are pretty proud. Bud, Jayne, Jeff and baby Kathy have moved to Evanston where they found an apartment big enough for the enlarged family and he reports his publishing venture is finally on its feet and doing splendidly.

Paul and I are finally settled in the new house and love it. It is small – one bedroom, a study with a bed – for Paul – and a dressing room, with a bed, for one, so we can turn the bedroom over to guests and yet we haven't a lot to take care of. The entrance patio, walled, with big plants, the living and dining area, the lanai (porch open on one side) and the lawn all open into each other with sliding glass doors so it is all one big living area open to breezes from the ocean which is half a block away. The kitchen is all electric – stove, garbage disposal, dishwasher, washing machine, lots of cabinet space and a big island work area sticking out in the middle. I have a minute Japanese gal who comes five days a week and gets breakfast, cleans the house, washes and irons and then goes away at noon, leaving us privacy. So you see it is all pretty comfortable. We love the people here and they have been very good to us. To sum it all up we are delighted with our choice of a house.

The way the St. Paul family travel about is fantastic* and sounds as if you were all having great fun. Only please travel this way.

Lots love,
Edith

This was the last letter Edith addressed to 'Betsy.' From now on she uses the nickname 'Betty.'

Edith questions why my mother was called 'Betty May.' Mom had been christened 'Eileen Mary Hopkins,' but her grandmother – who held the family purse strings – insisted on the nickname. Later, in 1965, when my mother divorces my father, she will switch to 'Eileen.'

*Regarding Edith's comments about Betty's family traveling, Leila explained that she herself had gone off to Pakistan from 1949 to 1950 and that her aunt and uncle, Lesley and Linda Ames, were in India the same year.

January 31, 1951
Honolulu

28 NIUHI STREET
WAILUPE PENINSULA
HONOLULU, HAWAII

Jan 31 – '51

Dear Non and Betty

Thanks for your letter and all its good news. That about Jim Turner
[Betty's nephew]* *was fine. He was evidently in love when he was here and
it's good to hear that his engagement and his arm are doing well. I don't
know when we have been so taken with anyone.*

*Mr. Freeburg was a little cagey over the phone when Paul called him;
evidently not wanting to get stuck with a couple of old bores. But they
dropped in one afternoon and we had a fine time and they stayed and
stayed and finally insisted we go out to a Chinese dinner with them. We had
to water the garden first so they pitched in and helped and then we spent
the evening together. We hope to see more of them when they get back from
the other islands.*

*The hope that you and Bet may be here before too long is grand. We
hope you will stay with us. We are a bit out of town but we can always
give you the use of a car and it would be such fun. When I read of the
weather you are having I should think you would hurry up. We are having*

a succession of cloudless sunny days with the thermometer in the eighties during the day but needing a blanket at night. When you come you will see why we are so mad about the place.

My love to you both – and the gals if they are at home—
Edith

---

*Leila noted, "Jim Turner, my first cousin, was engaged to Frances Black. They had loved each other since teenagers. She was from a Cincinnati family.

May 31, 1951
Honolulu

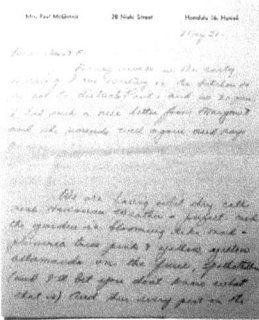

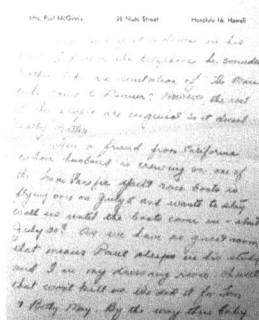

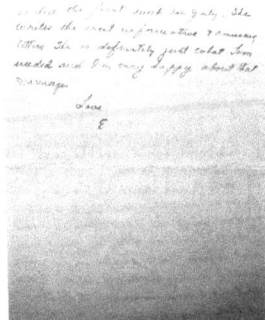

Edith wrote this letter to her Aunt E (Edith Theodora Ames Crosby, Betty's half-aunt), who was still living in Yarmouth, Massachusetts. Aunt E and Raymond will eventually move to Sante Fe, New Mexico, for Raymond's health, but he will die soon after. When Edith states that Tom and Betty May's baby is due the first week in July, she is talking about me. I arrived a bit earlier on June 23.

MRS. PAUL MCGINNIS – 28 NIUHI STREET
HONOLULU 16, HAWAII

May 31

Dear Aunt E:

Being awake in the early morning I am writing in the kitchen so as not to disturb Paul – and so no pen. [The letter is written in pencil.] *I had such a nice letter from Margaret and she sounds well again and says …* [the rest of the sentence has been erased].

We are having what they call real Hawaiian Weather – perfect – and the garden is blooming like mad – plumeria trees pink & yellow, yellow allamanda on the fence, spothothelum (and I'll bet you don't know what that is) and there is every pest in the world comes up and takes a bite. Yesterday was anti-pest day here. I soaked the ground with a solution that is supposed to destroy slugs & beetles. I sprayed everything with "Black Leaf 40" – which is supposed to get everything else. And I'll bet they will all be up nibbling again tonight. But in spite of it all we are getting rather nice.

Just at present we are rather over run with mainland friends. Two of mother's pals are here but are definitely trying not to encroach. But they are so nice I want to see them. – Clifton Webb, the actor is with us. I haven't seen him but he called up and so I am giving a dinner on Tuesday and he is so strange that I haven't any idea whether he and his very vulgar mania will show up. He says it is down in his book but over the telephone he sounded rather like an imitation of "The Man Who Came to Dinner." However, the rest of the people are congenial so it doesn't really matter.

Then a friend from California whose husband is crewing on one of the Trans Pacific yacht race boats is flying over on July 5 and wants to stay with us until the boats come in – about July 20th. As we have no guest room that means Paul sleeps in his study and I in my dressing room – oh well, that won't kill us. We did it for Tom & Betty May. By the way their baby is due the first week in July. She writes the most informative & amusing letters. She is definitely just what Tom needed and I'm very happy about that marriage.

Love.

E

Spring, 1952
Pasadena, California

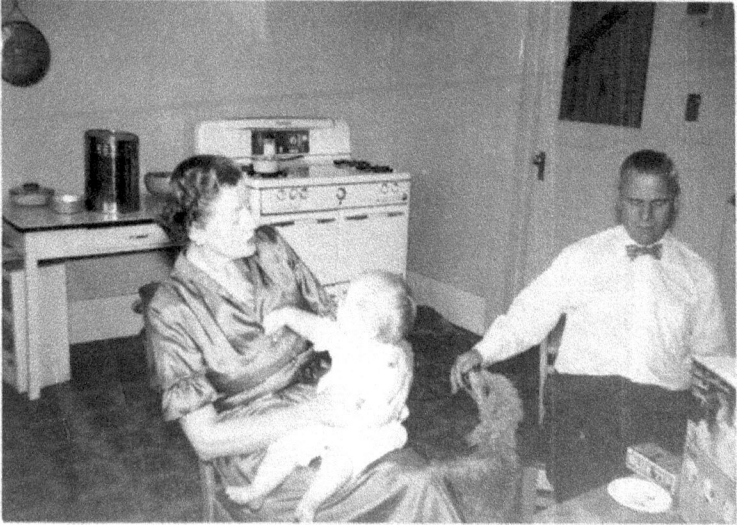

Edith and Paul traveled to Pasadena to visit my family when I was about one, as you can see from the photo of them with me above. We are in the kitchen of the house my family called 'The Big House' and which the newspapers dubbed the 'Purple Cow House.' It stood on the corner of Woodland Road and El Molino in Pasadena. We moved from The Big House to a small Victorian at 305 Ramona Avenue in Sierra Madre a couple of years later after my brother Tom (Thomas Winter Ames Jr.) was born on September 13, 1952, and before my brother Charles (Charles Hopkins Ames) was born on March 1, 1955.

Summer, 1955
Sierra Madre, California

My mother was always very fond of Edith. My father must have taken this photo in the back yard of our Sierra Madre house on a warm summer day. Mom hangs on to my brother Tommy while our Grandma Edith embraces me and our baby brother Charlie.

1957
Sierra Madre, California

The only one-on-one event I remember spending with my grandmother was when she took me to Bullock's Department Store, the fashionable place to shop in Pasadena in those days, and where my mother would not take me because it was "too expensive." It was 1957. I was six. I wore white gloves and Grandma wore kid gloves that matched her purse. We ate lunch in Bullock's tea room after picking out a linen dress for me with flowers appliquéd to the front. I never had the opportunity to wear it. My mother probably took this photo of us standing in the front patio of our home in Sierra Madre at 305 Ramona Avenue.

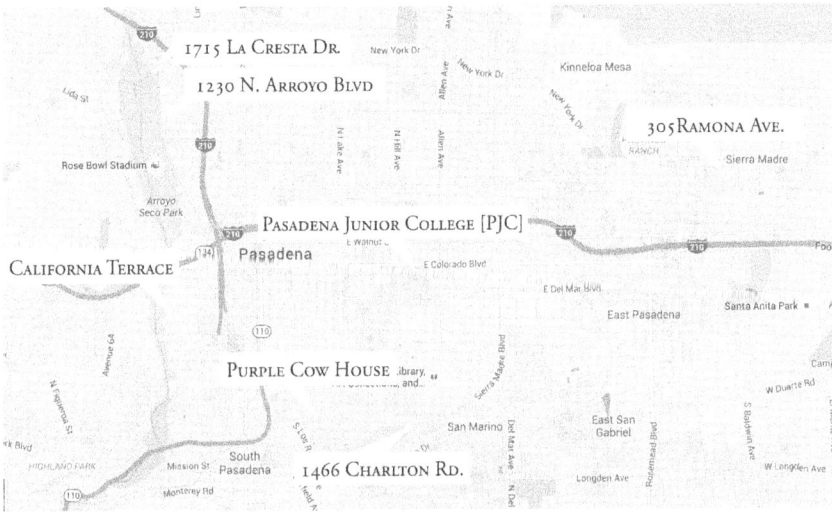

Edith's oldest son, Bud, still lived in the Chicago area. He and his wife, Jayne, had three children by this time: Jeffrey Knowlton Ames (Jeff), Katherine Skirm Ames (Kathy) and Elizabeth Winter Ames (Liz). The middle brother, Bob, with his wife, Kay, lived in Yakima, Washington. They had two girls by 1957: Robin Louise Ames and Marta Lesley Ames. The youngest of the grandchildren, Haven Winter Ames, did not arrive until later.

San Francisco and Carmel Valley

―――⟶∞∞⟵―――

I took the above photo of my Grandma and Grandpa-Paul's apartment on the corner of Laguna (left) and Jackson (right) in San Francisco circa 1960. I can't remember whether their apartment was the top or the middle floor.

April 17, *probably* 1960
San Francisco, California

I do not know why or exactly when Edith and Paul moved from Hawaii to San Francisco, but I remember visiting them at their new apartment when I was about nine, so it was around 1960. I was impressed by the modern wall-to-wall carpet and how everything was a light color – the carpet, the walls and the furniture. A silver rimmed crystal cigarette holder packed with cigarettes and a matching silver lighter were the only items on a large coffee table in front of the sofa. My grandmother was not into clutter. She smoked cigarettes constantly. Paul usually held a pipe in his hand. A few years after Edith writes this letter, Paul will require an invasive operation to remove cancer in his jaw because of that pipe.

2107 Jackson St. San Francisco
April 17th

Dear Betty & Non:
I hear from Les that you and Alice will be going to Santa Fe [to see Aunt E] on May 7th and I'm glad because perhaps you can help with a problem of Aunt E's. Her x-rays showed the bone mending nicely and they hope she will be on crutches in another six weeks. But she is still at Miss Averys because (she says) of the problem of finding suitable help at home. There is decided friction between Miss Avery (who, in spite of her great kindness to Aunt E. is a very domineering woman) and Aunt E's invaluable nurse Mrs. Riley – who does not like homecare cases and only took this out of affection for Aunt E. The friction was visible when I was there and must have increased because now Aunt E. has become aware of it. Mrs. McComb

has done everything to fix the house for Aunt E's return and I do wish something could be done to get her moved. I don't know what you can do but I thought if you were aware of the situation before you arrived it might help.

Do you plan to come on to San Francisco? We want so much to see you. We planned to drive to Yakima some time in May to see Bob and his family and if we knew if and when you would be here, we could arrange our schedule.

This is such a lovely town. It's a bright sunny Easter and the window in front of my desk looks down steep Laguna St. to the blue bay where a destroyer is messing about and there's lots of little white sails.

Love to you both.
Edith

My mother took a frustratingly short 8mm movie during our visit to San Francisco to see them. I viewed it recently after ordering the films digitized. Mom captured our family walking up one of San Francisco's steep hills. Grandma Edith was holding my hand. It made me feel good to see her demonstration on that film and in the photos of our family above. I hope when my brothers and cousins read this compilation, they will feel that warmth, too.

Leila took her husband and children, Betty's grandchildren, to see her Great-Aunt E in Santa Fe in September of 1957. "We found her living at the Posada Apartments," she told me.

Close to that time my father took our family to visit her as well. Aunt E was also his great-aunt. She was in her ninety-ninth year. He must have known she was on her last legs and wanted us children to meet her.

I remember my great-great-aunt Edith sitting in a dark room, in a dark chair, dressed in black. It seemed to me she was the oldest person in the world. We had not been in the house long before she gave me an assignment. She handed me a piece of paper and her family Bible and told me to copy her/our family lineage to two passengers who sailed to America on the *Mayflower* in 1620 – Richard Warren and Francis Cooke. Not until decades later did I appreciate how important it was to her to pass that information on to me. Her mother, Fanny Baker, began the application process for proving the line with the Mayflower Society back in the 1890s. The process got stuck for Fanny when she tried to find a family link for people who lived in upstate New York before proper vital records were kept there. A hundred years later, a friend of mine, Pat Friesen – who is now the Governor of the California Mayflower Society – figured out how to close the link and helped me get the line approved.

A funny thing is that my grandfather Junior was also a descendant of Francis Cook, but through a different daughter. Junior and Edith were ninth cousins. I doubt they knew that.

April 20, 1965
Carmel Valley, California

Edith and Paul moved once again, this time to a retirement community in Carmel Valley, California. Edith is seventy years old. Paul was sixty-nine.

MRS. PAUL MCGINNIS
HACIENDA CARMEL, CARMEL, CALIFORNIA

April 20

Dear Betty & Non:

Paul died on April 11th. We were driving south to see Tom and Betty May and had stopped for lunch in Buellton where they serve a pea soup which Paul especially liked, and which he enjoyed that day. Going back to the car he stumbled and I saw he was sick and sat him down on a nearby wall and yelled for someone to get a doctor and an ambulance. There was a doctor just going in to lunch and he did everything he could but I think Paul was gone before the ambulance came about five minutes later. They tried oxygen in the ambulance and adrenalin and heart massage at the hospital but it was no use. Thank goodness I don't think he felt any pain. He just looked surprised for a moment and then was unconscious.

According to what we had agreed on I had his remains cremated in Santa Barbara [forty-four miles south of Buellton along Highway 101] *the next day and the ashes shipped to the cemetery in Minneapolis for further instructions. I plan to go east sometime late in May or early June for a simple ceremony and interment.*

I tried to reach Les by phone but there was no answer, so I suppose he is still abroad. I sent a letter with instructions on the envelope for his secretary to open it and forward the information.

My children have wanted to come here but there is nothing they can do and they all have various commitments of their own lives to attend to. Frankly I want to be alone until I can catch up with myself. The outflow of kindness here at the Hacienda is unbelievable and my next door neighbor is caring for me like a mother. So there is nothing you can do that isn't being done. I just have to pick myself up. And will hope to see you in a month or so. Bud and his son Jeff want to come on to the memorial services. Also Bob – and, I suppose – Tom. Can you take us all in at 501 [Grand Avenue]?

Love – Edith

August 30, 1965

Four months later, Edith died in her residence at the Hacienda Carmel at 9:45 in the morning. Cause of death: "Prob. Suicide, Self administered overdose of Nembutal."

Uncle Bud, who was still living in Chicago, must have been the first one notified. "K. Lyman Ames (son)" was listed as the informant. He immediately flew to Carmel to take care of things.

My mother told me that she received the phone call about Edith's death and passed the information on to my father. "He cried bitterly," she said.

I remember being stunned. I was fourteen. My parents had just announced they were getting divorced and were moving into separate houses. Paul, the warmest and coziest of my grandparents – even though he was only a step – had died only a few months earlier. Edith was the only grandmother I met or knew. My mother's mother died when my mother was a little girl.

I had always been told my grandmother suffered from alcoholism, but I did not learn about the cause of her death until a decade later.

Final Thoughts

---◈◈◈---

For as long as I can remember, a pastel portrait of Edith hung in my bedroom, probably because I was her namesake. It was painted in 1900 when she was five and before the shooting of her brother Gilbert. It still hangs over my bed. I have always wondered why she looks so sad.

After reading these letters, I feel I better understand my grandmother. For one thing, unlike my father, who was interested in everything in life except, ironically, football, it does not appear that my grandmother had other interests besides the men in her life and her cousin Betty. She played golf with Paul, but never on her own. Her interest in gardening seems to have been a phase. Her sons and grandchildren were scattered around the country.

I imagine that if Edith were to give me one piece of advice today, it would be to "be useful." Edith liked being useful. She felt fulfilled in her nursing assignment during World War I. In her letters to her mother from France, she seemed happy. But in the rest of her letters, she seemed desperately lonely.

Betty, in contrast, kept active doing social work in St. Paul. In 1947, she and her sister Margaret were decorated with the Order of the British Empire for their service during World War II. Betty's daughters suspect she suffered from depression, but she had loads of family around her for support.

Edith was cremated and her ashes buried in the Lakewood Cemetery in Minneapolis alongside her brother Gilbert, their parents Alice and Tom, her husband Paul, her Aunt E, her grandfather Charles Gordon Ames, her grandmother Fanny Baker and her great-grandmother Julia Canfield Baker. She is not alone now.

Betty lived another twenty-five years. This photo of her with her husband, Norris Jackson, was taken on their fiftieth wedding anniversary in 1972. They held the ceremony at 501 Grand.

An award certificate sent to me by their daughter Leila stated that the Grand Hill Gang (their neighborhood in St. Paul) gave them the "highest honors in the renewing, recycling, and renovating for the Grand Hill Area." Norris lived in the community longer than any. With his wife, he resided in more houses; renovated more things and recycled more ideas and people.

The award read: "We, the people and friends of this neighborhood extend our appreciation for [their] continued rehabilitation of our community and our lives."

———— ⊗⊗⊗ ————

A color version of this book is available on Amazon for the Kindle.
More family stories by Mary Ames Mitchell are
available on Amazon.com as print books and in ebook format for the
Kindle and iBooks.

•

The Man in the Purple Cow House: and Other Tales of Eccentricity
includes the story of Edith Ames Winter Ames McGinnis' first husband,
Knowlton Lyman Ames, Jr.

•

The Search for My Abandoned Grandmother:
A genealogical journey unveils secret love stories and family mysteries
is about Mary's maternal grandmother,
Eileen Maud Thomas Hopkins Armitage.

———— ⊗⊗⊗ ————

I encourage you to leave comments or ask questions via my website
www.MaryAmesMitchell.com
Thank you for sharing this story with me.

www.ingramcontent.com/pod-product-compliance
Lightning Source LLC
Chambersburg PA
CBHW070802280326
41934CB00012B/3022